系列

麦格希 中英双语阅读文库

一生必读的名著
World-Famous Book V
第辑

[英]Kenneth Grahame　[英]Harry Gilbert ◎著　　　刘永佳　刘庆双◎译

吉林出版集团有限责任公司

图书在版编目(CIP)数据

一生必读的名著. 第 5 辑 : 英汉对照 / (英) 格雷厄姆 (Grahame,K.) , (英) 吉尔伯特 (Gilbert,H.) 著 ; 刘永佳, 刘庆双译. -- 长春 : 吉林出版集团有限责任公司, 2012.9

(麦格希中英双语阅读文库)

ISBN 978-7-5534-0606-0

Ⅰ.①一… Ⅱ.①格… ②吉… ③刘… ④刘… Ⅲ.①英语－汉语－对照读物 Ⅳ.①H319.4

中国版本图书馆 CIP 数据核字(2012)第 221480 号

一生必读的名著 第 5 辑

著 :	(英)Kenneth Grahame	(英)Harry Gilbert
翻 译 :	刘永佳	刘庆双
插 画 :	齐 航	李延霞
责任编辑 :	沈丽娟	孟广霞
封面设计 :	李立嗣	

开　本 : 650mm×960mm　1/16

字　数 : 226 千字

印　张 : 10

版　次 : 2013 年 1 月第 1 版

印　次 : 2015 年 4 月第 3 次印刷

出　版 : 吉林出版集团有限责任公司

发　行 : 吉林出版集团外语教育有限公司

地　址 : 长春市泰来街 1825 号

邮编 : 130011

电　话 : 总编办 : 0431-86012683

发行部 : 0431-86012675　0431-86012826(Fax)

网　址 : www.360hours.com

印　刷 : 北京一鑫印务有限责任公司

ISBN 978-7-5534-0606-0　定价 : 29.80 元

前 言

英语思想家培根说过：阅读使人深刻。阅读的真正目的是获取信息，开拓视野和陶冶情操。从语言学习的角度来说，学习语言若没有大量阅读就如隔靴搔痒，因为阅读中的语言是最丰富、最灵活、最具表现力、最符合生活情景的，同时读物中的情节、故事引人入胜，进而能充分调动读者的阅读兴趣，培养读者的文学修养，至此，语言的学习水到渠成。

"麦格希中英双语阅读文库"在世界范围内选材，涉及科普、社会文化、文学名著、传奇故事、成长励志等多个系列，充分满足英语学习者课外阅读之所需，在阅读中学习英语、提高能力。

◎难度适中

本套图书充分照顾读者的英语学习阶段和水平，从读者的阅读兴趣出发，以难易适中的英语语言为立足点，选材精心、编排合理。

◎精品荟萃

本套图书注重经典阅读与实用阅读并举。既包含国内外脍炙人口、耳熟能详的美文，又包含科普、人文、故事、励志类等多学科的精彩文章。

◎功能实用

本套图书充分体现了双语阅读的功能和优势，充分考虑到读者课外阅读的方便，超出核心词表的词汇均出现在使其意义明显的语境之中，并标注释义。

鉴于编者水平有限，凡不周之处，谬误之处，皆欢迎批评教正。

我们真心地希望本套图书承载的文化知识和英语阅读的策略对提高读者的英语著作欣赏水平和英语运用能力有所裨益。

丛书编委会

Contents

The Adventures of Tom Sawyer

Chapter 1 The Fence

Tom Sawyer lived with his aunt because his mother and father were dead. Tom didn't like going to school, and he didn't like working. He liked playing and having *adventures*. One Friday, he didn't go to school—he went to the river.

Aunt Polly was angry. "You're a bad boy!" she said. "Tomorrow

---

汤姆索亚历险记

第一章 栅栏

汤姆索亚和他姨妈住在一起，因为他的母亲和父亲都死了。汤姆不想去上学，他也不喜欢工作。他喜欢玩和冒险。一个星期五，他没有去学校——他去了河边。

波莉姨妈很生气。"你是个坏孩子！"她说。"你明天不能和你的朋

---

adventure *n.* 冒险

you can't play with your friends because you didn't go to school today. Tomorrow you're going to work for me. You can paint the *fence*."

Saturday morning, Tom was not happy, but he started to paint the fence. His friend Jim was in the street.

Tom asked him, "Do you want to paint?"

Jim said, "No, I can't. I'm going to get water."

Then Ben came to Tom's house. He watched Tom and said, "I'm going to swim today. You can't swim because you're working."

Tom said, "This isn't work. I like painting."

"Can I paint, too?" Ben asked.

友玩，因为你今天没去上学。明天你将要为我工作。你可以漆栅栏。"

星期六早晨，汤姆不高兴，但是他还是开始漆栅栏。他的朋友吉姆就在街上。

汤姆问他，"你想油漆吗？"

吉姆说，"不，我不能。我要去拿水。"

然后本来到汤姆的家里。他看着汤姆说，"我打算今天去游泳。你不能游泳因为你得工作。"

汤姆说，"这不是工作。我喜欢油漆。"

"我也可以油漆吗？"本问。

---

fence *n.* 栅栏

"No, you can't," Tom answered. "Aunt Polly asked me because I'm a very good *painter*."

Ben said, "I'm a good painter, too. Please, can I paint? I have some fruit. Do you want it?" "OK," Tom said. "Give me the fruit. Then you can paint."

Ben started to paint the fence. Later, many boys came to Tom's house. They watched Ben, and they wanted to paint, too.

Tom said, "Give me some food and you can paint."

Tom stayed in the yard, and the boys painted. They painted the

---

"不，你不能，"汤姆回答说。"波莉姨妈要我做，因为我是一个很好的油漆匠。"

本说，"我也是一个很好的油漆匠。求求你了，我可以油漆吗？我有一些水果。你想要吗？"好吧，"汤姆说。"给我水果。然后你就可以油漆了。"

本开始漆栅栏。后来，许多男孩来到汤姆的家。他们看着本，并且他们也想油漆。

汤姆说，"给我一些吃的，你们就可以油漆了。"

汤姆待在院子里，这些孩子们在油漆。他们油漆了栅栏三次。栅栏很

---

painter *n.* 油漆匠

fence three times. It was beautiful and white.

Tom went into the house. "Aunt Polly, can I play now?" he asked.

Aunt Polly was surprised. "Did you paint the fence?" she asked.

"Yes, I did," Tom answered.

Aunt Polly went to the yard and looked at the fence. She was very *surprised* and very happy. "It's beautiful!" she said. "Yes, you can play now."

Tom walked to his friend Joe Harper's house and played with his friends there. Then he walked home again. There was a new girl in one yard. She had yellow hair and blue eyes. She was beautiful. Tom wanted to talk to her, but she didn't see him. She went into her house. Tom waited, but she didn't come out again.

漂亮也很白。

汤姆走进了房里。"波莉姨妈,我现在可以玩了吗?"他问。

波莉姨妈很惊讶。"你油漆栅栏了吗?"她问。

"是的,我油漆完了,"汤姆回答说。

波莉姨妈跑到院子里,看着栅栏。她很惊讶也很高兴。"真漂亮!"她说。"好的,你现在可以玩了。"

汤姆走到他的朋友乔·哈珀的家里,并和他的朋友在那里一起玩耍。之后他又走回了家。他发现有一个他不认识的女孩在一个院子里。她有黄色的头发和蓝色的眼睛。她很漂亮。汤姆想和她说说话,但女孩没看见他。她走进她的房子。汤姆就等着,但她再也没有出来过。

---

surprised *adj.* 惊讶的

Chapter 2 In the Graveyard

One morning before school, Tom's friend Huck Finn waited for him in the street. Huck didn't have a home, and he never went to school. People in the town didn't like him. But Tom liked Huck.

Huck said, "Let's have an adventure."

"What can we do on our adventure?" Tom asked.

"Let's go to the *graveyard* at night—at twelve o' clock!" Huck answered.

"That's a good adventure," Tom said. "Let's meet at eleven o'clock."

第二章 在墓地

一天早上上学之前，汤姆的朋友哈克·费恩在街上等着他。哈克没有家，他也从不去学校。镇上的人都不喜欢他。但是汤姆喜欢哈克。

哈克说，"我们去冒险吧。"

"我们冒险去做什么？"汤姆问。

"我们晚上去墓地——十二点！"哈克回答。

"这是一个很好的冒险，"汤姆说。"我们十一点见面吧。"

---

graveyard *n.* 墓地

Then Tom went to school, but he was late. The teacher was angry. He asked, "Why are you late again?"

"I'm late because I talked to Huck Finn," Tom said.

Then the teacher was very angry. "Sit with the girls," he said to Tom.

Tom sat near the beautiful new girl. He was happy. He looked at her.

"What's your name?" he asked.

"Becky," she answered.

Tom smiled and said, "My name's Tom."

The teacher was angry again. "Tom Sawyer, stop talking! Go to your *place* now," he said. Tom went to his place.

然后汤姆去了学校，但是他迟到了。老师很生气，问道，"你为什么又迟到了？"

"我来迟了，是因为我和哈克说话了，"汤姆说。

听完之后老师非常生气。"和女孩们坐在一起，"他对汤姆说。

汤姆坐在一个他不认识的漂亮女孩旁边，他很开心。他看着她。

"你叫什么名字？"他问。

"贝基，"她答道。

汤姆笑着说，"我叫汤姆。"

老师又一次生气了。"汤姆·索亚，不要说话！现在去你的位子，"

---

place *n.* 座位

At twelve o'clock Tom and Becky didn't go home. They stayed in the school yard and talked. Tom said, "I love you. Do you love me?"

"Yes," Becky answered.

"Good," Tom said. "Then you're going to walk to school with me every day. Amy always walked with me."

"Amy!" Becky said angrily. "Do you love her?"

"No," Tom answered. "I love you now. Do you want to walk with me?"

But Becky *was angry with* Tom. She walked away and didn't answer. Tom was unhappy. He didn't go to school in the afternoon.

他说。汤姆就坐在了他的地方。

十二点了，汤姆和贝基没有回家。他们待在学校的院子里说话。汤姆说，"我喜欢你，你喜欢我吗？"

"喜欢，"贝基回答。

"太好了，"汤姆说。"以后你要和我一起每天步行去学校。艾米总是跟我一起走。"

"艾米！"贝基生气地说。"你喜欢她吗？"

"不，"汤姆说。"我现在喜欢你。你想跟我一起走吗？"

但是贝基对汤姆很生气。她没有回答就走了。汤姆很不高兴。他下午

---

be angry with 生……的气

That night Tom went to bed at nine o'clock, but he didn't sleep. At eleven o'clock he went out of his bedroom window to the yard. Huck was there. They walked to the graveyard. They stopped behind some big trees and talked quietly.

Suddenly, there was a noise. Three men came into the graveyard— the doctor, Muff Potter, and Injun Joe. Injun Joe and the doctor talked angrily. Then Injun Joe killed the doctor with a knife.

Tom and Huck watched. Then they went away quickly because they were afraid.

没有去上学。

那天晚上，汤姆九点上床睡觉，但是他没有睡着。他十一点从卧室窗户出去，来到院子里。哈克就在那里。他们走到了墓地。他们在一些高大的树木后面停下并轻声地交谈着。

突然，有个声音。三个人走进了墓地——一名医生，莫夫·波特和印第安·乔。印第安·乔和医生愤怒地交谈。然后，印第安·乔用刀杀了医生。

汤姆和哈克看见了。然后他们迅速离开了，因为他们很害怕。

---

suddenly *adv.* 突然地

They went to Tom's *yard*. Huck said, "We can't talk about this. Injun Joe can find us and kill us, too."

"That's right," Tom said. "We can't talk about it."

Tom went in his bedroom window. He went to bed, but he didn't sleep well. Tom and Huck didn't talk to their friends or Aunt Polly about that night because they were afraid of Injun Joe.

Later, some men went to Muff Potter and said, "You're a bad man. You killed the doctor."

他们去了汤姆的院子。哈克说，"我们不能谈论这个。印第安·乔也可以找到我们，并杀死我们的。"

"没错，"汤姆说。"我们不能谈论这件事。"

汤姆从窗户进了卧室。他上床睡觉，但是他并没有睡好。汤姆和哈克没和他们的朋友或波莉姨妈谈论那晚发生的事情，因为他们害怕印第安·乔。

后来，一些人去找莫夫·波特说，"你是个坏男人。是你杀了医生。"

---

yard *n.* 院子

Chapter 3 A Bad Day

Becky was sick and didn't go to school for many days. Tom was very sad. One morning, he said to Aunt Polly, "I'm very sick, and I want to stay home from school."

Aunt Polly said, "Here's some *medicine*. Take this and you can get well quickly."

But Tom didn't like the medicine. Peter, the cat, came into the room and looked at Tom.

"Peter!" Tom said. "Have some medicine!"

第三章 糟糕的一天

贝基生病了，好几天都没有去上学。汤姆很伤心。一天早上，他跟波莉姨妈说，"我很不舒服，我想待在家里不去学校。"

波莉姨妈说，"这有一些药。喝了它们，你可以很快恢复健康。"

但汤姆不喜欢吃药。彼得———一只猫，走进了房间，看着汤姆。

"彼得！"汤姆说。"吃些药吧！"

---

medicine *n.* 药

Peter had some medicine. He didn't like it! He went quickly out of the open window and into the yard.

Aunt Polly watched Peter. "Why did you do that, Tom?" she asked *angrily*. "You're a very bad boy! Go to school now."

Tom arrived at school early and he waited for Becky at the school fence. She arrived early, too, but she didn't look at Tom. She went into school. Tom walked away. He didn't want to go to school now. He was very sad.

Joe Harper was near the school. He was sad, too, because his mother was angry with him. The two boys walked and talked.

彼得就吃了这些药。他不喜欢它！他很快从敞开的窗口出来到了院子里。

波莉姨妈看到彼得。"你为什么这么做，汤姆？"她生气地问。"你是个坏男孩！现在去上学。"

汤姆很早就到了学校，并且在学校的围墙边等着贝基。她也早就到了，但她没有看见汤姆。她走进了学校。汤姆离开了，他现在不想去上学了。他很伤心。

乔·哈珀在学校附近。他也很伤心，因为他的妈妈对他很生气。这两个孩子边走边聊着。

---

angrily *adv.* 生气地

MCGRAW-HILL

Tom said, "Let's *run away*."

"Yes, let's!" Joe said.

The two boys went to the river. Huck Finn was there. Tom and Joe said, "We're going to run away. Do you want to come with us?"

"Yes," Huck answered. "Let's go across the river. We can have a good adventure there."

The boys went home because they wanted to get food for their adventure.

汤姆说，"我们逃走吧。"

"好的，我们走！"乔说。

这两个孩子来到河边。哈克·费恩也在那里。汤姆和乔说，"我们要逃走，你想和我们一起去吗？"

"好的，"哈克说。"咱们过河吧。在那儿，我们可以经历一次很好的冒险。"

这些孩子们都回家了，因为他们都想为他们的冒险带上些食物。

---

run away 逃跑

Chapter 4 Across the River

Tom, Joe, and Huck went to the river. There was a small boat there. The boys went across the river in the small boat. They said, "This is a good place because we can play all day. There's no school here."

They played and then went to sleep.

In the morning, the boys were happy again. They said, "Let's stay here for a long time."

In the afternoon, they played near the river again. Suddenly, there was a *noise* from a big boat on the river. The boys stopped playing and watched the boat.

第四章 过河

汤姆，乔和哈克来到了河边，在那儿有一艘小船。这些孩子们乘小船过了河。他们说："这是个不错的地方，因为我们可以玩一整天。这儿没有学校。"

他们玩着玩着就睡着了。

到了早晨，男孩们又很高兴。他们说，"让我们在这里待很长一段时间。"

到了下午，他们又在河边玩耍。突然，从河面上的一个大船传来一个声音。男孩们不玩了，看着船。

noise *n.* 声音

"Listen," Tom said. "The men on the boat are talking about us."

The boys listened *quietly*. A man said, "The boys are in the river. They're dead."

Tom said, "Those men are looking for us in the river. We're here, but they don't know that."

That night, the boys were sad. Huck and Joe went to sleep, but Tom didn't sleep. He went home in the small boat. He quietly went in his bedroom window. Then he went under his bed and stayed there.

Aunt Polly and her friends came into his room. Aunt Polly said to her friends, "Tom was a good boy, and I loved him. Now he's dead, and I'm very sad."

"听着，"汤姆说。"船上的人们在谈论我们。"

男孩们静静地听着。有人说，"这些孩子掉到河里了。他们已经死了。"

汤姆说，"那些人是在河里寻找我们。我们在这里，但他们不知道。"

当晚，男孩们有些伤心。哈克和乔去睡觉了，但汤姆没有睡着。他乘小船回到家中。他悄悄地从窗户进了卧室。然后他来到床下并待在那里。

波莉姨妈和她的朋友们来到他的房间。波莉姨妈对她的朋友们说，"汤姆是个好孩子，我很爱他。现在他死了，我很难过。"

---

quietly *adv.* 静静地

Tom wanted to say, "I'm not dead." But he stayed quiet.

Aunt Polly went to sleep. Tom went out of the window very quietly and went back across the river.

In the morning, Joe and Huck said, "We're not happy here now. We want to go home."

Tom said, "Let's go home on Sunday. We can *go to church*. People are going to be very surprised!"

Sunday morning, many children were at church. They talked about the three boys. They were sad because their friends were dead. Becky was sad, too.

Suddenly, the three boys walked into the church. People were very surprised, but they were very happy, too.

汤姆想说，"我没死。"但是他还是没出声。

波莉姨妈去睡觉了。汤姆悄悄地从窗户出去过了河。

早晨，乔和哈克说，"我们现在在这里不快乐。我们想要回家了。"

汤姆说，"我们星期日回家。我们可以去教堂做礼拜。人们将会很惊讶！"

星期日早上，许多孩子都在做礼拜。他们谈论着三个男孩。他们感到难过，因为他们的朋友都死了。贝基也很伤心。

突然，这三个男孩走进教堂。人们都很惊讶，但他们还是很高兴。

---

go to church　（去教堂）做礼拜

Chapter 5 At School

Monday morning, Tom went to school. The children wanted to hear about his adventure, and Tom liked talking about it. Becky wanted to talk to Tom, but he didn't look at her.

Then Tom talked to Amy. Becky watched him and she was angry. She said to her friends, "I'm going to have an adventure day. You can come on my adventure." But she didn't ask Tom.

Later in the morning, Tom talked to Amy again. Becky talked to her friend Alfred and looked at a *picture-book* with him. Tom watched them and he was angry with Becky.

In the afternoon, Tom waited for Becky at the school fence. He

---

第五章 在学校

星期一上早晨，汤姆去上学。孩子们想听听他的冒险经历，汤姆也愿意谈谈这次经历。贝基想和汤姆说话，但是汤姆并没有看着她。

后来汤姆跟艾米说话。贝基看着他，生气了。她对她的朋友说，"我想要去冒险一天。你们可以加入我的冒险。"但她没有问汤姆。

过了早上，汤姆又和艾米说话了。贝基和她的朋友艾尔弗雷德交谈着，同时和他看着一本漫画书。汤姆看着他们，他对贝基很生气。

到了下午，汤姆在学校的围墙边等着贝基。他说，"我很抱歉。"

---

picture-book *n.* 漫画书

said, "I'm sorry."

But Becky didn't listen to him. She walked into the school room. The teacher's new book was on his table. This book wasn't for children, but Becky wanted to look at it. She opened the book quietly and looked at the pictures.

Suddenly, Tom came into the room. Becky was surprised. She closed the book quickly, and it *tore*. Becky was angry with Tom and quickly went out of the room.

Then the children and the teacher came into the room and went to their places. The teacher looked at his book.

"Who did this? Who tore my book?" he asked angrily.

The room was very quiet. The teacher started to ask every child, "Did you do this?"

但是贝基没有听他说的话，她走进了教室。老师的新书放在桌子上。这本书不是给孩子们看的，但贝基想去看看。她打开书静静地看着这些图片。

突然，汤姆走进了房间。贝基很惊讶。她很快地合上书，它被撕破了。贝基对汤姆很生气，并迅速地走出了房间。

后来孩子们和老师走进房间并走到自己的位子。老师看着他的书。

"这是谁干的？谁把我的书撕了？"他生气地问。

教室里很安静。老师开始问每个孩子，"是你这样做的吗？"

---

tear *v.* 撕碎

They answered, "No, I didn't."

Then he looked at Becky. "Becky, did you do this?"

Tom wanted to help her. Suddenly he said, "I did it. I tore your book."

"Tom Sawyer, you're a very bad boy. Stay here after school!" the teacher said angrily.

At five o'clock Tom started to walk home. Becky *waited for* him at the school fence. "You're a very good friend," she said.

Tom smiled at her and they walked home.

他们回答，"不，我没有。"

然后他看着贝基。"贝基，是你这样做的吗？"

汤姆想要帮助她。突然，他说，"我做的，是我把你的书撕了。"

"汤姆·索亚，你是个坏男孩。放学后留在这里！"老师生气地说。

到了五点，汤姆开始步行回家。贝基在学校的围墙边等着他。"你是我的一个很好的朋友，"她说。

汤姆朝她笑笑，然后他们一起走回家。

wait for　等候

Chapter 6 The Trial

Summer vacation started, and Becky went away with her family. Tom was unhappy.

Then Muff Potter's *trial* started. Tom and Huck remembered the night in the graveyard. They were afraid of Injun Joe again.

"Did you talk about the night in the graveyard?" Tom asked Huck.

"No, I didn't," Huck answered. "Did you?"

"No," Tom answered. "But I'm sorry about Muff Potter. He's always friendly to us. He didn't kill the doctor. I want to help him."

第六章 审判

暑假开始了，贝基和她的家人离开了。汤姆很不开心。

莫夫·波特的审判开始了。汤姆和哈克记得在墓地的那个晚上。他们又很害怕印第安·乔。

"你谈论过墓地的那个晚上吗？"汤姆问哈克。

"不，我没有，"哈克说。"你呢？"

"没有，"汤姆说。"但是我对莫夫·波特感到很抱歉。他总是对我们很友好。他没有杀那个医生，我想帮助他。"

trial *n.* 审判

"Let's take some food to him," Huck said.

The boys *visited* Muff Potter. "Here's some food," they said.

Muff Potter said, "Thank you. You're good boys."

Tom and Huck went to the trial and listened for two days. Tom didn't sleep well at night because he wanted to help Muff Potter.

On the third day of the trial Tom talked.

A man asked him, "Where were you on the night of June 17th?"

"I was in the graveyard," Tom answered.

"Did you see any people there?" the man asked.

"Yes. Injun Joe, the doctor, and Muff Potter were there. They didn't see me because I was behind some big trees."

"让我们给他带一些吃的吧，"哈克说。

男孩们见到了莫夫·波特。"这里有一些食物，"他们说。

莫夫·波特说，"谢谢，你们是好孩子。"

汤姆和哈克去听了两天的审判。汤姆晚上没有睡好是因为他想帮助莫夫·波特。

在第三天审判时汤姆说话了。

一个人问他，"6月17日的晚上你在哪里？"

"我在墓地，"汤姆回答。

"你在那里看到什么人了吗？"那人问。

"是的。印第安·乔，医生，和莫夫·波特在那里。他们没有看到我

---

visit *v.* 拜访

"What did you see?" the man asked.

"Injun Joe and the doctor talked angrily," Tom answered. "Then Injun Joe killed the doctor with his knife. Muff Potter didn't do it."

The people at the trial were surprised. Injun Joe quickly went out of the building.

Tom and Huck were very afraid. Tom said, "Now Injun Joe knows about us. He can kill us, too."

Many people wanted to hear about the boys' adventure in the graveyard. Tom liked talking about it. He was happy, too, because he helped Muff Potter. But he didn't sleep well because he *was afraid of* Injun Joe.

是因为我在一些大树后面。"

"你看到了什么？"那人问。

"印第安·乔和医生愤怒的交谈，"汤姆说。"然后，印第安·乔用他的刀杀了医生。莫夫·波特并没有这样做。"

审判厅的人们感到很惊讶。印第安·乔迅速走出了审判厅。

汤姆和哈克都非常害怕。汤姆说，"现在印第安·乔知道我们了。他也会杀了我们的。"

很多人想听听男孩们在墓地的冒险。汤姆愿意谈论这件事。他也很高兴，因为他帮助了莫夫·波特。但是他没睡好，因为他害怕印第安·乔。

---

be afraid of 害怕

Chapter 7 Injun Joe's Treasure

One Saturday afternoon, Tom wanted to have an adventure because he didn't want to think about Injun Joe. He went to Huck and said, "I'm going to look for *treasure*. Do you want to come with me?"

Huck always liked an adventure. "Oh, yes," he said. "Where can we look?"

"Let's start looking in the old house near Mrs. Douglas's house. Old houses are good places for treasure," Tom answered.

The boys went to the old house. They wanted to look at every

第七章 印第安·乔的宝藏

一个星期六的下午，汤姆想要进行一次冒险，因为他不愿意去想印第安·乔。他找到哈克说，"我要去寻找宝藏。你想跟我一起吗？"

哈克总是喜欢冒险。"噢，好的，"他说。"我们在哪里可以找到呢？"

"让我们首先在道格拉斯太太房子附近的老房子里看看吧。老房子是放宝藏的好地方，"汤姆回答。

男孩们去了老房子。他们想看看每个房间。首先他们到厨房去了，然

---

treasure *n.* 宝藏

room. First they went into the kitchen, and then they went into the bedroom.

Suddenly, two men came into the *kitchen* —Injun Joe and his friend. The boys were afraid and stayed in the bedroom very quietly.

Injun Joe walked across the kitchen. "We can put our money here," he said to his friend.

He started to dig under the floor with his knife.

"What's this?" Injun Joe said. "I'm going to get it out."

There was a big box under the floor. He opened it with his knife. There was a lot of money in the box.

"Look at that money!" his friend said. "Let's go now. We can come back and get it tomorrow."

后他们走进了卧室。

突然，两个人走进了厨房——印第安·乔和他的朋友。孩子们很害怕并非常安静地待在卧室里。

印第安·乔穿过厨房。"我们可以把钱放在这里，"他对他的朋友说。

他开始用刀挖着地板。

"这是什么？"印第安·乔说。"我快把它挖出来了。"

在地板下面有一个大箱子。他用刀撬开了它。在大箱子里有很多的钱。

"看看这些钱！"他的朋友说。"咱们现在走吧。我们可以明天再来拿。"

---

kitchen *n.* 厨房

"No," Injun Joe said. "We're going to take it with us now. We can take it to that place. You know—the place under the *cross*."

Then the men went out of the house. Injun Joe talked quietly to his friend. The boys listened and were afraid.

Tom said, "Did you hear that? He wants to kill us."

They went out of the house quietly and went home.

The boys were afraid of Injun Joe, but they wanted to find his treasure. They watched his house every night, but they didn't see Injun Joe or his treasure.

"不，"印第安·乔说。"我们现在要拿走它。我们可以把它带到那个地方。你知道的——在十字架下面。"

然后这些男子走出了房子。印第安·乔静静地和他的朋友交谈着。孩子们听着，都很害怕。

汤姆说，"你听到了吗？他想杀了我们。"

他们静静地走出房子并回家去了。

男孩们对印第安·乔很害怕，但他们想找到他的宝藏。他们每天晚上都看着他的房子，但是他们没看见印第安·乔或他的宝藏。

---

cross *n.* 十字架

Chapter 8   Becky's Adventure Day

In August Becky's family came back from their *vacation*. Tom was very happy and he didn't think about Injun Joe's treasure.

Becky's adventure day was Saturday. Her mother said, "You can sleep at Susy Harper's house after your adventure."

"Good," Becky said.

Becky and her friends went on the river on a big boat. The boat went down the river and across it. Then it stopped. The children went out of the boat and played games near the river. In the afternoon one boy asked, "Who wants to go to the big cave?"

第八章 贝基一天的冒险

八月到了，贝基一家结束了他们的假期。汤姆非常高兴，他不去想印第安乔的宝藏了。

贝基的冒险日是星期六。她的母亲说，"你可以在冒险之后睡在苏西先生的房子里。"

"好的，"贝基说。

贝基和她的朋友们乘着一艘大船航行在河上。小船顺流而下，穿过了河。然后船停了。孩子们下了船，在河边玩游戏。下午，一个男孩问，"谁想去大洞穴？"

vacation *n.* 假期

The children went to the *cave*. It was dark and cold there, but they played games. In the evening they went back to the boat and went home.

Sunday morning, Becky's mother and Aunt Polly talked to Mrs. Harper at church. Becky's mother asked, "Where's my Becky? Did she sleep at your house?"

"No, she didn't," Mrs. Harper answered. "I didn't see her."

Aunt Polly said, "My Tom didn't come home. Did he stay at your house?"

孩子们就去了山洞。那儿又黑又冷，但他们玩着游戏。到了晚上他们返回到船上并回家了。

星期日早上，贝基的母亲和波莉姨妈在教堂里和哈帕太太说话。贝基的母亲问，"我的贝基在哪里？她睡在你的家里吗？"

"不，她没有，"哈帕太太回答。"我没看到她。"

波莉姨妈说，"汤姆也没有回家。他待在你家里了吗？"

---

cave *n.* 洞穴

"No, he didn't," Mrs. Harper answered.

Then Aunt Polly and Becky's mother asked the children, "Did Tom and Becky come home? Did you see them on the boat?"

The children answered, "No, we didn't see them, but it was dark."

Then a boy said, "Maybe they're in the cave!"

Two hundred men *looked for* Tom and Becky in the cave. They looked for three days, but they didn't find them. People in the town were very sad.

"不，他没有，"哈帕太太回答。

然后波莉姨妈和贝基的母亲向孩子们询问，"汤姆和贝基回家了吗？你们在船上看到他们了吗？"

孩子们回答说，"不，我们没有看到他们，但是天已经黑了。"

然后一个男孩说，"也许他们在洞穴里！"

二百个人在洞穴里寻找着汤姆和贝基。他们找了三天，但没有找到他们。镇上的人都很伤心。

---

look for 寻找

Chapter 9 Huck's Adventure

Huck didn't go on Becky's adventure. He stayed home and watched Injun Joe's house that night. At eleven o'clock Injun Joe and his friend came out and walked *down* the street. There was a box in his friend's hands.

Huck said quietly, "Maybe that's the treasure box." He went after the two men.

They walked to Mrs. Douglas's house and stopped in her yard. Huck stayed behind some small trees. The men talked, and Huck listened to them.

第九章 哈克的冒险

哈克不想继续贝基的冒险。他那天晚上待在家，监视印第安·乔的房子。晚上十一点钟，印第安·乔和他的朋友出来了，沿着街道走着。他的朋友的手里拿着一个箱子。

哈克默默地说，"也许这就是宝藏箱。"他跟在那两个人的后面。

他们走在去道格拉斯太太家的路上，到了庭院的时候停了下来。哈克藏在一些小树后面。他们交谈着，哈克听着他们的谈话。

down *prep.* 沿着

Injun Joe was angry. "I want to kill her," he said to his friend. "Mr. Douglas was bad to me. He's dead now, but I remember."

"There are a lot of *lights* in the house. Maybe her friends are visiting," Injun Joe's friend said. "We can come back tomorrow."

"No," Injun Joe said. "Let's wait now."

Huck liked Mrs. Douglas because she was always good to him. He wanted to help her. He quietly walked away and then he started to run to Mr. Jones's house.

Mr. Jones opened the door. "What do you want?" he asked Huck.

"Injun Joe and his friend are in Mrs. Douglas's yard," Huck said. "They want to kill her. Can you go there and help Mrs. Douglas?"

印第安·乔很生气。"我要杀了她，"他对他的朋友说。"道格拉斯先生对我不好。他现在死了，但是我仍然记得。"

"房子里亮着很多盏灯。也许她有朋友来访，"印第安·乔的朋友说。"我们可以明天再来。"

"不，"印第安·乔说。"我们等吧。"

哈克喜欢道格拉斯太太，因为她总是对他好。他想帮助她。他悄悄地走开了，然后他开始朝琼斯先生家的方向跑去。

琼斯先生打开门。"有什么事儿吗？"他问哈克。

"印第安·乔和他的朋友在道格拉斯太太的院子里，"哈克说。"他

---

light *n.* （电）灯

"Yes. My sons and I can go there," Mr. Jones answered. "You can go home."

In the morning, Huck went back to Mr. Jones's house.

"How's Mrs. Douglas?" he asked.

"She's OK," Mr. Jones answered. "The men went away because we *arrived*."

"Good," Huck said. But he was afraid of Injun Joe. "Please don't say my name to Mrs. Douglas."

Mr. Jones looked at him, and then he said, "You aren't well. Go and sleep in my bedroom."

们想杀了她。你可以去那里帮助道格拉斯太太吗？"

"是的。我的孩子，我可以去那里，"琼斯先生回答。"你可以回家了。"

大早上，哈克来到琼斯先生的家。

"道格拉斯太太还好吗？"他问。

"她很好，"琼斯先生回答。"当我们到达那里的时候，那两个男人就跑了。"

"太好了，"哈克说。但他怕印第安·乔。"请不要把我的名字告诉道格拉斯太太。"

琼斯先生看着他，然后接着说，"你看起来很不舒服。去我的卧室睡一会儿吧。"

---

arrive *v.* 到达

Later, Mrs. Douglas visited Mr. Jones.

"You helped me yesterday night. Thank you," she said. "You're a good man."

Mr. Jones said, "We didn't know about the men in your yard. A boy was there and he wanted to help you. He came here, but I can't say his name."

Mr. Jones and Mrs. Douglas went to church. People there talked about Tom and Becky. Mr. Jones and his sons went to the cave with the men, but on Monday morning they went home. Huck *was in bed* and was very sick. The men went back to the cave, but Mrs. Douglas stayed with Huck.

后来，道格拉斯太太来拜访琼斯先生。

"你昨天晚上帮助了我。谢谢你，"她说。"你是一个好人。"

琼斯先生说，"我们不知道这些男人出现在你的院子里。是一个男孩在那里，他想帮助你。他来到这里，但我不知道他的名字。"

琼斯先生和道格拉斯太太一同去教堂。在那里的人们都在谈论汤姆和贝基。琼斯先生和他的儿子和大家一起来到洞穴，但是在星期一早上他们回家了。哈克躺在床上，病得很严重。琼斯先生和他的儿子又回到洞穴，但道格拉斯太太留下来陪哈克。

---

be in bed　躺在床上

Chapter 10 In the Cave

Saturday, Tom and Becky walked and played in the cave. Then they stopped near some water.

"What time is it?" Becky asked.

"I don't know," Tom said. "Let's *go back* now."

The two children walked and walked. But they didn't find the door to the cave. Becky was afraid. She wanted to sit down and eat. "Maybe they're looking for us now," she said.

"Here's some food," Tom said. "Eat this and wait here. I'm going to look for the door."

Tom walked and walked. But he didn't find the cave door.

第十章 在洞穴

星期六，汤姆和贝基在洞穴里行走和玩耍。然后他们在附近有水的地方停了下来。

"几点了？"贝基问。

"我不知道，"汤姆说。"我们现在回去吧。"

两个孩子走啊走。但是他们没有发现洞穴的门。贝基感到害怕。她想坐下，吃点儿东西。"也许他们在找我们了，"她说。

"这有一些食物，"汤姆说。"你吃，在这里等我。我去找找门。"

汤姆走啊走。但是他没有找到洞穴的门。突然，有人靠近他。汤姆很

---

go back 回去

Suddenly, there was a man near him. Tom was afraid, but he stayed quiet. He looked at the man. It was Injun Joe!

Tom was very afraid and he made a noise. Injun Joe went away quickly. Tom went back to Becky, but he didn't talk to her about Injun Joe.

They were in the cave for three days. Tuesday, Becky didn't want to walk. Again Tom said, "Stay here. I'm going to look for the door."

This time he went to a new place. There was light there. He went to the light. It came from a small door in the cave.

Tom went out of the cave. Then he went back to Becky. "Come with me," he said. "We can *go out of* the cave now."

Tom and Becky went out of the cave. They were very happy. They

---

害怕，但是他保持安静。他看见了那个男人。那是印第安·乔！

汤姆非常害怕，他叫了一声。印第安·乔急忙逃跑了。汤姆回到贝基身边，但是他没有和她讲印第安·乔的事。

他们在洞中待了三天。星期二，贝基不想走。汤姆说，"待在这里。我去找门。"

这一次他来到了一个新的地方。这里有光。他朝亮光走去。这光是从洞上的一个小门照射进来的。

汤姆走出了洞，然后他回到贝基身边。"跟我来，"他说。"我们现在可以从洞中出去啦。"

汤姆和贝基走出了洞穴。他们很高兴。他们来到河边，在那里等一些人坐着小船来到他们面前。

---

go out of 出去

went to the river and waited there. Some men in a small boat came to them.

Tom said, "We want to go home. Can you help us?"

The men answered, "Yes. We can take you home."

Tom and Becky went in the boat with the men. They arrived home very late Tuesday night, and people in the town were very happy. Tom talked *all night* about their adventure in the cave.

汤姆说，"我们要回家，你能帮助我们吗？"

男人们回答，"是的。我们可以带你们回家。"

汤姆和贝基和那些人一同坐上了船。他们星期二晚上很晚才到家，镇上的人都很高兴。汤姆彻夜谈论他们在洞穴的冒险。

all night 整夜

Chapter 11 In the Cave Again

Tom and Becky stayed home for many days. Then, two weeks after their adventure, Tom visited Becky and talked to her father.

Mr. Thatcher said, "You're a very good boy, Tom. You helped Becky in the cave. Thank you. People can't go into it now because it has a new big door."

"But Injun Joe's living in the cave!" Tom said.

Some men went down the river to the cave. Tom went with them. They opened the new door. Injun Joe was there, but he was dead.

Tom wanted to *talk to* Huck. Later in the week he went to Mr.

第十一章 重入洞穴

汤姆和贝基在家待了许多天。于是，在他们的冒险结束两周后，汤姆来到贝基的家，把这个想法告诉了她父亲。

赛切尔先生说，"你是个好孩子，汤姆。你在洞中帮助了贝基。谢谢你。没有人能再次进入洞穴，因为它有一个新的大门。"

"但是印第安·乔生活在洞穴！"汤姆说。

一些人沿着河岸走向洞穴。汤姆和他们一同前去。他们打开了这扇新的大门。印第安·乔在那里，但是他已经死了。

汤姆想把这个消息告诉哈克。一周后他到来琼斯先生的家。这俩孩子

---

talk to 同（某人）谈话

Jones's house. The two boys talked about their adventures.

"The money isn't in Injun Joe's house," Tom said. "It's in the cave! I know, because Injun Joe was there. Let's get it!"

Huck was afraid. "But *maybe* we can't find it."

"I can find it again," Tom said. "I know about a small door at the back of the cave. Becky and I came out there. We can go in that door, and I can find Injun Joe's treasure."

"OK," Huck said. "Let's go today."

That afternoon the boys went in a small boat to the back of the cave. Tom walked first, and Huck went after him. They walked and walked.

谈论了他们的冒险。

"钱不在印第安·乔的房子里，"汤姆说。"一定在洞穴里！我知道，因为印第安·乔在那里。让我们把它拿到手！"

哈克很害怕。"但也许我们不能找到它。"

"我能再次找到它，"汤姆说。"我知道洞穴后面的一个小门。贝基和我从那里出来的。我们可以从那扇门进去，然后我可以找到印第安·乔的宝藏。"

"好的，"哈克说。"我们今天就去。"

当天下午，小男孩们坐小船到了后面的洞穴。汤姆在前面走，哈克在后面跟着。他们走啊走。

---

maybe *adv.* 也许

Then Tom said, "This is the right place! Injun Joe was here."

The boys looked for a good place for treasure.

Suddenly, Tom said, "Look! There's a cross! Injun Joe said, 'under the cross.' Let's look there!"

The boys went to the place with the cross. Tom said, "I'm going to *dig* here with my knife ... Look! It's the treasure box! Let's get it out now. The treasure's ours!"

"This box is very heavy," Huck said. "We can't take it with us."

"I have some small bags," Tom said. "We can put the money in them and take it home."

The boys went out of the cave with the money.

然后汤姆说，"就是这个地方！印第安·乔在这里。"

男孩们到处寻找能够藏宝的好地方。

突然，汤姆说，"看！这有一个十字架！印第安·乔说过，'在十字架下。'让我们到那里看看！"

男孩子们去到有十字架的地方。汤姆说，"我要在这里用刀挖一挖……看！是宝箱！让我们现在就把它挖出来。宝藏是我们的啦！"

"这箱子很重，"哈克说。"我们不能把它带走。"

"我有一些小袋子，"汤姆说。"我们可以把钱放在小袋子里带回家。"

男孩子们带着钱离开了洞穴。

---

dig *v.* 挖

Chapter 12 At Mrs. Douglas's House

Tom said, "Let's take the money to the old house near Mrs. Douglas's house. That's a good place for it."

They started to walk to the old house. Mr. Jones was in Mrs. Douglas's yard. He called to the boys.

"A lot of people are waiting for you. Come with me," he said. They *went into* Mrs. Douglas's house.

"Hello, boys," Mrs. Douglas said. "Come with me."

Tom and Huck went with her to a bedroom. There were new

第十二章 在道格拉斯太太家

汤姆说，"让我们把钱拿到道格拉斯夫人家附近的老房子里。这是一个藏钱的好地方。"

他们开始朝老房子走去。琼斯先生在道格拉斯太太的院子里。他向男孩们呼喊着。

"很多人都等着你。跟我来，"他说。他们一同来到道格拉斯太太的房子里。

"你好，小伙子，"道格拉斯太太说。"跟我来。"

汤姆和哈克跟她走到卧室。在床上放着新的衬衫和牛仔裤。

---

go into 进入

shirts and jeans on the bed.

"Wash your hands and faces and put on these shirts and *jeans*," Mrs. Douglas said. "Then come to the big room."

The boys went to the room. A lot of people were there.

Mrs. Douglas said, "First I want to say 'thank you' to Mr.Jones and his sons. They helped me. They're very good people."

"Huck helped, too," Mr. Jones said.

"Thank you, too, Huck," Mrs. Douglas said. "You're a good boy, and I like you. I want to give you a home and some money."

"洗洗你们的手和脸，把这些衬衫和牛仔裤穿上，"道格拉斯太太说。"然后到大房间里来。"

孩子们来到房间。很多人在那里。

道格拉斯太太说，"我想对琼斯先生和他的儿子们说'谢谢'。他们帮助了我。他们是非常好的人。"

"是哈克帮助了你，"琼斯先生说。

"也谢谢你，哈克，"道格拉斯太太说。"你是个好男孩！我喜欢你。我想给你一栋房子和一些钱。"

---

jeans *n.* 牛仔裤

"But Huck has a lot of money!" Tom said.

He went to the bedroom and came back with the bags of money. "We have this money from the cave. There's a lot of money in them, and it's ours now."

There was $12,000 in the bags. The people were very *surprised*. They asked about the boys' adventure.

"哈克有很多钱！"汤姆说。

他走进卧室，带回来的是一袋袋的钱。"我们从洞穴里得到这些钱。那里有很多钱，现在是我们的了。"

有12,000美元在袋里。人们都很惊讶。他们问了男孩子们的冒险。

---

surprised *adj.* 惊讶的

Chapter 13 Huck's New Home

Huck *lived in* the big house with Mrs. Douglas. He was a new person. He washed every day, and he went to school and church. But he wasn't happy. He stayed there for three weeks, and then he ran away.

Tom went to Huck. "Why did you run away?"

Huck answered, "Mrs. Douglas is a good woman. I like her, but I can't live with her. I don't like washing every day, and I don't like going to school and church. I don't want to have a lot of money. But I want to be your friend. OK?"

第十三章 哈克的新家

哈克和道格拉斯太太住在大房子里。他像变了一个人似的。他每天洗澡，去学校和教堂。但他不快乐。他在那里待了三个星期，然后他就跑了。

汤姆去找哈克。"你为什么要逃跑？"

哈克说，"道格拉斯太太是个好人。我喜欢她，但是我不能和她生活在一起。我不喜欢每天都洗澡，我不喜欢去学校和教堂。我不想有很多钱。但是我想成为你的朋友，好吗？"

live in 居住

"No," Tom said, "I can't be your friend, because the boys at school don't want to play with you. We're *thinking about* a lot of new adventures. Please live with Mrs. Douglas and come to school. Then the boys at school can play with you."

"I want to be your friend," Huck said, "and I want to have adventures with you and the boys at school. Maybe I can live with Mrs. Douglas. I don't know, but I'm going to try it again for a month."

"Good," Tom said. "The boys are meeting later, at twelve o'clock at night. You can come, too."

"Good!" Huck said.

"不，"汤姆说，"我不能成为你的朋友，因为学校里的男孩们不想跟你玩。我们考虑着许多新的冒险。请你和道格拉斯太太住在一起，去上学。然后学校的男孩们会和你一起玩的。"

"我想成为你的朋友，"哈克说，"我想与你和学校的男孩子们继续新的冒险。也许我能和道格拉斯太太住在一起。我不知道，但是我愿意再次尝试一个月。"

"好的，"汤姆说。"男孩们打算晚点儿聚会，在晚上十二点。你也过来呀。"

"好的！"哈克说。

---

think about 考虑

02

The Adventures of Huckleberry Finn

Chater 1 Huck in Trouble

You don't know about me if you haven't read a book called *the Adventures of Tom Sawyer*. Mr Mark Twain wrote the book and most of it is true. In that book *robbers* stole some money and hid it in a very secret place in the woods. But Tom Sawyer and I found it, and after that we were rich. We got six thousand dollars each all gold.

哈克贝利·费恩历险记

第一章 哈克遇到麻烦

如果你没有看过《汤姆·索亚历险记》那本书，你就不知道我。这本书是马克·吐温写的，大部分是真实的。在那本书中，强盗们偷了钱，并把钱藏在了树林中一个秘密的地方。但我和汤姆·索亚找到了这笔钱，在这之后，我们发财了。我们每个人得到了6000美元——全是金币。

robber *n.* 强盗

In those days I never had a home or went to school like Tom and all the other boys in StPetersburg. Pop was always *drunk*, and he moved around a lot, so he wasn't a very good father. But it didn't matter to me. I slept in the streets or in the woods, and I could do what I wanted, when I wanted. It was a fine life.

When we got all that money, Tom and I were famous for a while. Judge Thatcher, who was an important man in our town, kept my money in the bank for me. And the Widow Douglas took me to live in her house and said I could be her son.

She was very nice and kind, but it was a hard life because I had to wear new clothes and be good all the time.

In the end, I put on my old clothes and ran away. But Tom came

---

在那些日子里，我从来没有一个家，或是像汤姆和圣彼得斯堡所有其他的男孩那样去上学。爸爸总是喝得醉醺醺的，经常转来转去，所以，他不是一个很好的父亲。但是，这对我来说无所谓。我睡在街上或林子里，只要我想做，我就能做我想做的事情。这真是一种美好的生活。

当我和汤姆得到那些钱时，我们出了一阵子名。撒切尔法官是我们镇子上的一个重要人物，他替我将钱存在了银行。道格拉斯寡妇领我到她家去住，并说我可以做她的儿子。

她非常和蔼，但这是一种令人难以忍受的生活，因为我不得不穿新衣服，而且始终都要听话。

最后，我穿上我的旧衣服跑掉了。可汤姆追上了我说，我得回去，但

---

drunk *adj.* 喝醉的

after me and said that I had to go back, but that I could be in his gang of robbers. So, I went back, and the widow cried and I had to put on those new clothes again. I didn't like it at all. Her sister, Miss Watson, lived there too. She was always saying, "Don't put your feet there, Huckleberry," and "Don't do that, Huckleberry." It was terrible.

When I went up to bed that night, I sat down in a chair by the window. I sat there a good long time, and I was really unhappy. But just after midnight I heard "mee-yow! mee-yow!" outside. Very softly, I answered, "mee-yow! mee-yow!" Quietly, I *put out* the light and got out through the window. In the trees, Tom Sawyer was waiting for me.

We went through the trees to the end of the widow's garden.

我仍可以加入他的强盗团伙。所以，我回去了，寡妇叫着，我不得不又穿上那些新衣服。我根本不喜欢这一切。她的姐姐沃森小姐也住在那儿。她总是说，"别把你的脚放在那儿，哈克贝利，"还有"别干那个，哈克贝利。"真是糟透了。

那天晚上，上床睡觉的时候，我坐在窗边的椅子上。我坐了很久，真是很难受。但是，午夜刚过，我听到外面"喵！喵！"的声音。我很轻地回答着"喵！喵！"。我轻轻地吹灭蜡烛，从窗户爬了出去。汤姆·索亚正在树丛中等我。

我们穿过树丛来到寡妇的花园的尽头。不一会儿，我们就到了房子

---

put out　熄灭

Soon we were on top of a hill on the other side of the house. *Below* us we could see the river and the town. One or two lights were still on, but everything was quiet. We went down the hill and found Joe Harper, Ben Rogers and two or three more of the boys. Then Tom took us down the river by boat to his secret place, which was a cave deep in the side of a hill. When we got there, Tom told us all his plan.

"Now, we'll have this gang of robbers," he said, "and we'll call it Tom Sawyer's Gang. If somebody hurts one of us, the others will kill him and his family. And if a boy from the gang tells other people our secrets, we'll kill him and his family, too."

另一头的一个小山顶上。我们能看到山下的小河和镇子。一两处烛光仍亮着，但是，万籁俱寂。我们下了山，找到了乔·哈珀，本·罗杰斯，还有两三个其他的男孩。然后，汤姆用船把我们带到了那个秘密的地方，这个秘密的地方是山坡深处的一个岩洞。当我们到那时，汤姆把他的全部计划告诉了我们。

"现在，我们就来组织这个强盗团伙，"他说，"我们就叫它汤姆·索亚团伙吧。如果有人伤害我们中的某个人，其他的人就要杀了他和他的全家。如果这个团伙的哪个男孩把我们的秘密告诉了其他人，我们也要把他和他的全家都给杀喽。"

below *prep.* 在……下面

We all thought this was *wonderful*, and we wrote our names in blood from our fingers. Then Ben Rogers said, "Now, what's the gang going to do?"

"Nothing," replied Tom. "Just rob and kill. We stop people on the road, and we kill them, and take their money and things. But we can keep a few of the people, and then their friends can pay money to get them back. That's what they do in the stories in books."

But Ben wasn't happy. "What about women?" he asked. "Do we kill them, too?"

"Oh, no," Tom answered. "We're very nice to them, and they all

---

我们都觉得棒极了，我们用手指上的血写上了我们的名字。然后，本·罗杰斯说，"这团伙到底要干些什么呢？"

"什么都不干，"汤姆回答道，"只是抢劫和杀人，我们在路上拦截人，杀了他们，拿走他们的钱和东西。但是，我们可以留下几个人，这样，他们的朋友可以交钱把他们赎回去。这就是人们在书中故事里所做的。"

但是，本不高兴了。"女人怎么办？"他问道，"我们也杀她们吗？"

"噢，不，"汤姆回答。"我们对她们很友好，她们都爱我们，她们

---

wonderful *adj.* 极好的

love us, and they don't want to go home."

"Then the cave will be full of women, and people waiting, and we'll have to watch them all night..."

"We'll all go home now," Tom said, "and we'll meet next week, and we'll kill somebody and rob somebody."

Ben wanted to begin on Sunday, but the others said no. It was bad to kill and rob on a Sunday.

My clothes were very dirty and I was very tired when I got back. Of course, the next morning Miss Watson was angry with me because of my dirty clothes, but the *widow* just looked unhappy. Soon after that we stopped playing robbers because we never robbed people and we never killed them.

不想回家。"

"那么，岩洞里全都是女人，人们等待着，我们将不得不整夜监视她们……"

"我们现在都回家吧，"汤姆说，"我们下周碰头，杀个什么人，抢劫个什么人。"

本想星期天开始，但是，其他的人不同意。星期天杀人抢劫是不好的。

我回来时，衣眼很脏，我也很疲倦。第二天早晨，当然是因为我的脏衣服，沃森小姐很生我的气，可寡妇只是看上去不高兴。之后不久，我们就不玩强盗的游戏了，因为，我们从来没抢劫过人，从来没杀过人。

---

widow *n.* 寡妇

Time went on and winter came. I went to school most of the time and I was learning to read and write a little. It wasn't too bad, and the widow was pleased with me. Miss Watson had a slave, an old man called Jim, and he and I were good friends. I often sat talking to Jim, but I still didn't like living in a house and sleeping in a bed.

Then, one morning, there was some new snow on the ground and outside the back garden I could see *footprints* in the snow. I went out to look at them more carefully. They were Pop's footprints!

A minute later, I was running down the hill to Judge Thatcher's house. When he opened the door, I cried, "Sir, I want you to take all my money. I want to give it to you."

　　时间流逝，冬天来到了。大部分时间我去学校上学，我学认字，也学着写一点。还好，寡妇对我挺满意。沃森小姐有一个奴隶，是个叫吉姆的老头，我和他是好朋友。我经常坐下来和他聊天，但我仍然不喜欢住在房子里，睡在床上。

　　后来，一天早晨，地上刚刚覆盖了一层雪，我能够看见外边后花园雪中的脚印。我出去更加仔细地察看，是爸爸的脚印！

　　片刻之后，我跑下山来到了撒切尔法官家。他打开门时，我叫喊着，"先生，我要你把我的钱都拿去。我想把钱送给你。"

---

footprint *n.* 脚印

He looked surprised. "Why, what's the matter?"

"Please, sir, take it! Don't ask me why!"

In the end he said, "Well, you can sell it to me, then." And he gave me a dollar and I wrote my name on a piece of paper for him.

That night when I went up to my room, Pop was sitting there, waiting for me! I saw that the window was open, so that was how he got in.

He was almost fifty and he looked old. His hair was long and *dirty* and his face was a terrible white colour. His clothes were old and dirty, too, and two of his toes were coming through his shoe. He looked at me all over for a long time, and then he said, "Well, just look at those clean, tidy clothes! And they say you can read and write now. Who said you could go to school?"

他看上去很惊讶。"嗨，怎么回事？"

"先生，请收下！不要问我为什么！"

最后，他说，"好吧，你可以卖给我。"他给了我一张美元，我在一张纸上为他写上了我的名字。

那天晚上，当我走进我的房间时，爸爸坐在那儿，正在等我！我看见窗户是开着的，所以，他是从窗户进来的。

他差不多50岁了，显得很老。他的头发又长又脏，脸色白得可怕。他的衣眼也又旧又脏，两个脚指头从鞋里露了出来。他久久地上下打量着我，然后说道，"噢，就看看这些干净、整齐的衣服吧！他们说你现在能认字、写字了。谁说你可以上学了？"

---

dirty *adj.* 肮脏的

"The widow..." I began.

"Oh, she did, did she? Well, you can forget about school. I can't read and your mother couldn't read; no one in our family could read before they died, so who do you think you are? Go on, take that book and read to me!"

I began to read, but he hit the book and it flew out of my hand, across the room. Then he shouted, "They say you're rich—how's that?"

"It isn't true!"

"You give me that money! I want it. Get it for me tomorrow!"

"I haven't got any money. Ask *Judge* Thatcher. He'll tell you. I haven't got any money."

"寡妇……"我开始说。

"噢，她说的，是吗？好吧，你可以不提学校。我不认字，你妈妈不认字；咱们家人一直到死，都没有人认字，所以，你觉得你挺不错吧？拿起那本书，给我念念！"

我开始念，但是，他把书从我手中打掉了，打到了房间那头。然后，他喊道，"他们说你发财了——那是怎么回事？"

"那不是真的！"

"你把钱给我！我要钱。明天给我把钱拿来！"

"我没有钱。问问撒切尔法官。他会告诉你。我没有钱。"

---

judge *n.* 法官

"Well, give me what you've got in your pocket now. Come on, give it to me!"

"I've only got a dollar, and I want that to..."

"Give it to me, do you hear?"

He took it, and then he said he was going out to get a drink. When he was *outside* the window, he put his head back in and shouted, "And stop going to that school, or you know what you'll get!"

The next day he was drunk, and he went to Judge Thatcher to get my money. The judge wouldn't give it to him. But Pop didn't

---

"好吧，把你口袋里的钱给我。快点，把钱给我！"

"我只有一美元，我想用它去买……"

"把钱给我，你听见没有？"

他拿走了钱，然后说，他要去喝一杯。到了窗外时，他把头伸了回来，叫喊道，"别再去那个学校了，否则你清楚你会得到什么！"

第二天，他喝醉了，他去了撒切尔法官家去要我的钱。法官没给他。但是，爸爸不停地去要钱，每隔几天，我就从法官那儿拿两三美元给爸

---

outside *prep.* 在……外面

stop trying and every few days I got two or three dollars from the judge to stop Pop from hitting me. But when Pop had money, he got drunk again and *made trouble* in town. He was always coming to the widow's house, and she got angry and told him to stay away. Then Pop got really angry and one day he caught me and took me a long way up the river in a boat. I had to stay with him in a hut in the woods and I couldn't go out by myself. He watched me all the time. The widow sent a man to find me and bring me home, but Pop went after him with a gun, and the man ran away.

爸，免得他打我。但是，爸爸有钱时，就喝醉酒，在镇上惹麻烦。他总是到寡妇的家来，寡妇很气愤，让他走开。一天，爸爸真生气了。他抓住了我，带我坐船前行了很长一段路。我不得不和他待在树林中的一个小木屋里，我不能独自外出。他一直监视着我。寡妇派了个人找我，要把我带回家，可是，爸爸拿了支枪跟在后面，那个人吓跑了。

make trouble 惹麻烦

Chater 2 Huck Escapes and Finds a Friend

Mostly it was a lazy, *comfortable* kind of life, but after about two months Pop began to hit me too much with his stick. He often went away into town too, and then he always locked me in the hut. Once he was away for three days and I thought I was never going to get out again.

When he came back that time, he was drunk and angry. He wanted my money, but Judge Thatcher wouldn't give it to him. The judge wanted to send me to live with the widow again, Pop told me. I wasn't very pleased about that. I didn't want to go back there.

第二章 哈克出逃并找到一个朋友

大多数时候过着一种懒散、舒适的生活，但是，大约两个月后，爸爸开始更加狠命地用棍子打我。他也经常离开小木屋到镇上去，那时，他总是把我锁在小木屋内。有一次，他走了三天，我想，我永远也出不去了。

那次他回来时，醉醺醺的，而且还很生气。他想要我的钱，但撒切尔法官不给他。爸爸告诉我，法官想把我送去再和寡妇住在一起。我对此不太高兴。我不想回那儿去。

---

comfortable *adj.* 舒适的

So I decided to escape and go down the river and live in the woods somewhere. When Pop was out, I began to cut a hole in the wooden wall of the hut. In a few days, when the hole was bigger, I could take the wood cut, *escape* through the hole, and put the wood back.

One morning Pop sent me down to the river to catch some fish for breakfast. To my surprise, there was a canoe in the water and there was no one in it. Immediately, I jumped into the river and brought the canoe to the side. It was lucky that Pop didn't see me, and I decided to hide the canoe under some trees and use it when I escaped.

That afternoon, Pop locked me in and went off to town. "He won't be back tonight, " I thought, so I began to work hard at my

---

所以，我决定逃走，顺流而下，住在森林里的什么地方。爸爸出去的时候，我开始在小木屋的木墙上挖洞。过不了几天，洞大些的时候，我就可以把木头拿开，从洞里逃走，然后把木头放回去。

一天早晨，爸爸打发我到河里去抓鱼当早餐。令我吃惊的是河里有一只独木舟，里面没有人。我立即跳进河里，把独木舟带到了岸边。幸运的是爸爸没看见我，我决定把独木舟藏在树下，等我逃跑时好用。

那天下午，爸爸把我锁在屋里到镇上去了。我想，"他今晚不会回来了，"所以，我开始拼命挖洞。不久，我就能钻出去了。我带上食品、饮料和爸爸的枪上了独木舟。然后，我把那块木头放回去把洞掩盖起来，

---

escape *v.* 逃走

hole. Soon I could get out through it, and I carried food and drink and Pop's gun down to the canoe. Then I put back the wood to hide the hole, took the gun and went into the woods. There I shot a wild pig and took it back to the hut with me. Next, I broke down the door with an *axe*. I carried the pig into the hut and put some of its blood on the ground. Then I put some big stones in a sack and pulled it along behind me to the river. Last of all, I put some blood and some of my hair on the axe. I left the axe in a corner of the hut and I took the pig down to the river.

"They won't know it's only a pig in the river," I said to myself. "They'll think it's me."

Then I took the canoe and went down the river to Jackson's Island. By then it was nearly dark, so I hid the canoe under some

---

拿上枪，进了林子。在森林里，我开枪打死了一只野猪，把它带回了小木屋。接着，我用斧子把门劈开，拖着猪进了小木屋，在地上弄了些猪血。然后，我在袋子里放了些大石头，拽着袋子一直到了河边。最后，我在斧子上弄了些血和我的头发。我把斧子丢在小木屋的一个墙角，把猪扔到了河里。

"他们不会知道河里的东西只是一头猪，"我自言自语道。"他们会以为那是我。"

然后，我坐着独木舟，顺流而下来到杰克逊岛。那时候，天快黑了，所以，我把独木舟藏在树下，然后睡觉了。

---

axe *n.* 斧子

trees and went to sleep.

It was after eight o'clock when I woke up the next day and the sun was high in the sky. I was warm and comfortable and I didn't want to get up. Suddenly, I heard a noise up the river. Carefully, I looked through the trees, and I saw a boat full of people. There was Pop, Judge Thatcher, Tom Sawyer and his Aunt Polly and his brother Sid, and lots of others. They were looking for my body in the river. I watched them, but they didn't see me, and in the end they went away. I knew that *nobody* was going to come and look for me again. I found a good place under the trees to sleep and to put my things. Then I caught a fish and cooked it over a fire.

I lived like that for three days, and then I decided to look round the island. So I went into the woods. "This is my island," I thought.

第二天当我醒来时，已是八点多了，太阳已高高挂在天空。我感觉暖融融的，很舒服，我不想起来。突然，我听到河上游一阵喧闹声。我透过树丛仔细观看，看见一艘挤满人的船。船上有爸爸、撒切尔法官、汤姆·索亚和他的波莉姨妈，还有汤姆的弟弟锡德以及许多其他的人。他们在河里寻找我的尸体。我看着他们，可他们没看见我。最后，他们走了。我知道不会有人再来找我了。我在树下找了个睡觉、放东西的好地方。然后，我抓到了一条鱼，在火上烤了。

我在岛上就这样生活了三天，然后，我决定到岛上转一转。我进了森林。"这是我的岛，"我想，"我是这岛上唯一的人。"

---

nobody *pron.* 没有人

"I'm the only person on it."

Suddenly, just in front of me, I saw a fire, and it was still smoking. There was somebody on my island! I didn't wait. I turned and went straight back. But I couldn't sleep. After a time, I said to myself, "I can't live like this. I must find out who it is."

Silently, I moved along the river in my canoe, under the darkness of the trees. And then I stopped. Through the trees I could see the light of a fire. Afraid, I left my canoe and went nearer. There was a man lying by the fire. Suddenly, he sat up and I saw that it was Jim, Miss Watson's slave! I was really happy to see him! "Hello, Jim," I cried, and I jumped out from behind the tree.

Jim fell to his knees. "Please don't hurt me!" he cried. "I've always been good to dead people!"

突然，就在我面前，我看见了一堆火，仍然冒着烟。我的岛上还有别人！我一刻没停，转过身来，径直回到原地。但我睡不着觉。过了一段时间，我自言自语道，"我不能这样的生活下去。我必须弄清楚它是谁。"

我坐在独木舟里，借着树的黑暗，轻轻地顺流而下。然后，我停了下来。透过树丛，能看见一处火光。我胆战心惊地离开了独木舟，靠近火堆。有个人躺在火边。突然，他坐了起来，我看见那人是吉姆，沃森小姐的奴隶！看见他，我真高兴！"你好，吉姆，"我喊道，从树后跳了出来。

吉姆跪了下来。"请别伤害我！"他叫道。"对死去的人，我一直总是友好的！"

---

silently *adv.* 静静地

"It's all right, Jim. I'm not dead," I said. "But why are you here on the island?" I asked.

"Well, Huck," he began. "Old Miss Watson wanted to sell me. A man came into town and told Miss Watson that he'd buy me for eight hundred dollars. She couldn't say no, so I ran away. I ran down to the river to hide, but everybody in the town was there. They said you were dead, Huck. I had to wait all day to get away. When it was dark, I got on to a big boat and hid. When we came near this island, I jumped into the water and swam here."

Jim finished his story and then we both carried all our things into a cave and hid the *canoe* under some trees. We were just in time because then the rains came. It rained for days, and the river got higher and higher. All kinds of things came down the river and

---

"没事儿，吉姆。我没死，"我说。"可你为什么在这个岛上呢？"我问。

"唉，哈克，"他开始道。"老沃森小姐想要卖我。一个男人来到镇上告诉沃森小姐，他要花800美元买我。她答应了，所以，我就逃了。我跑到河边藏了起来，可镇上所有的人都在那儿。他们说你死了，哈克。我不得不等上一整天再逃走。天黑时，我上了一条大船，藏在那儿。当我们靠近这个岛时，我跳进水里，游到了这儿。"

吉姆讲完了他的经历，然后，我们俩把我们所有的东西都搬到了一个岩洞里，把独木舟藏在树下。我们刚干完，雨就下起来了。雨接连下了数

---

canoe *n.* 独木舟

one night there was a little wooden house, lying half on its side. We got the canoe out and went to take a look. Through the window we could see a bed, two old chairs and some old clothes. There was something lying in the corner and we thought it looked like a man. Jim went in to see, but he said, "He's dead. Someone shot him in the back. Don't look at his face, Huck. It's *terrible*!"

I didn't want to see the dead man's face, so I didn't look. We just took the old clothes and a few other things, and went back to our cave on the island.

Another night, when we were out looking for things on the river, we found a raft. It was made of good, strong wood, and was about four metres by five metres. "This could be useful," I said to Jim, so we pulled it back to the island behind the canoe, and tied it up under the trees.

日，河水越涨越高。各种各样的东西从河上漂了过来。一天夜里，有一座小木房子斜着浮在水面上。我们把独木舟弄出来，划过去看了看。透过窗户，我们看到一张床，两把旧椅子，还有一些旧衣服。屋角那儿躺着什么东西，看起来像个人。吉姆进去看了看，可他说，"他死了。有人在他的背后开了枪。别看他的脸，哈克。太可怕了！"

我根本不想看死人的脸，所以，我没看。我们拿了些旧衣服和一些别的东西，便回到了岛上的岩洞里。

又一天夜里，当我们出去寻找河上的东西时，我们发现了一个木筏子。它是由很好很结实的木头做成的，大约5米长，4米宽。"可能会有用的，"我对吉姆说。所以，我们把它拖在小木舟后带了回来，并把它拴在了树下。

---

terrible *adj.* 可怕的

Chater 3 Huck and Jim Travel South

For some days everything *went along* quietly, but we were getting bored. We wanted to know what was happening in town and so I decided to go and find out. Jim said, "Why don't you wear the old dress and the hat that we found in the house? People won't know you, then. They'll think you're a girl." And so I did.

Just after it was dark, I got into the canoe and went up the river to the bottom of the town. There, I left the canoe and went on foot.

第三章 哈克和吉姆向南旅行

几天来，一切都很顺利，但是，我们有点烦了。我们想知道镇上发生了什么事情，于是我决定去查清楚。吉姆说，"你为什么不穿上我们在那木房子里找到的旧衣服，戴上那帽子呢？那样，人们就不会认出你。他们会以为你是一个女孩呢。"于是，我照着他说的做了。

天刚黑，我上了独木舟，往上游划去来到镇边。我把独木舟留在那儿，步行前往。不久我来到了一座小房子前。这座小房子以前一直是空的，但现在里面有亮光，当我透过窗户往里望时，我看到了一位大约40

---

go along 进展

Before long, I came to a little house which was always empty. Now there was a light on, and when I looked through the window, I saw a woman of about forty. She was a stranger and that was good because she didn't know me. So I knocked on the door. "I must *remember* that I'm a girl," I said to myself.

The woman opened the door. "Come in," she said. She looked at me with her little bright eyes. "What's your name?" she asked.

"Sarah Williams," I replied. "I'm going to see my uncle, on the other side of town. My mother's ill, you see, and she needs help."

"Well, you can't go there by yourself now. It's too dark. My husband will be home in about an hour. Wait for him and he'll walk with you."

岁的女人。是个陌生人,这不错,因为她不认识我。所以,我敲了敲门。"我必须记住我是一个女孩儿,"我自言自语道。

那女人开了门。"进来吧,"她说道。她用她那小小的、亮亮的眼睛打量着我。"你叫什么名字?"她问道。

"萨拉·威廉斯,"我回答道。"我打算去见我的舅舅,他住在镇子的另一头。你瞧,我妈妈病了,她需要帮助。"

"噢,你现在不能自己去那儿。天太黑了。我丈夫大约一小时后会回来。等等他,他会跟你一起去的。"

---

remember *v.* 记得

And then she began to tell me about all her troubles. I was getting bored with all this until she said something about Pop and my *murder*.

"Who did it?" I asked.

"Well," she replied, "some people say old Finn did it himself; other people think it was a slave who ran away that night. His name was Jim. They'll give three hundred dollars to anybody who finds him—and they'll give two hundred dollars for old Finn. He got drunk and left town with two strangers. A lot of people think he killed his boy and he's going to come back one day, and get all Huck Finn's money." "And what about the slave?" I asked.

"Oh, they'll soon catch him. People want the three hundred dollars. I think he's on Jackson's Island, you know. I've seen smoke

---

　　然后，她开始对我讲起她的烦恼。对她所讲的这一切我变得厌烦了，直到她谈起爸爸和我的那件凶杀案。

　　"是谁干的？"我问道。

　　"嗯，"她回答道，"有人说是老费恩自己干的，其他的人认为是一个那天夜里逃走的奴隶干的。他的名字叫吉姆。他们出价300美元悬赏捉拿吉姆——并且他们出价200美元悬赏捉拿老费恩。他喝得醉醺醺的，和两个陌生人离开了镇子。许多人认为是他杀了他的儿子，有朝一日，他会回来，并且会得到哈克·费恩所有的钱。""那奴隶怎么样了？"我问道。

　　"噢，他们不久就会抓住他的。人们想要那300美元。我想，他在杰克逊岛上，我看到了那里有烟。我丈夫去找他的两个朋友，今夜晚些时

---

murder *n.* 谋杀

there. My husband's gone to get two of his friends and they're going over there with a gun later tonight."

When I heard this, my hands began to shake. The woman looked at me *strangely*, but then she smiled and said kindly, "What did you say your name was?"

"M-Mary Williams."

"Oh," she said, "I thought it was Sarah."

"Er… well, yes, it is. Sarah Mary Williams. Some people call me Sarah and some people call me Mary, you see."

"Oh, do they?" She smiled again. "Come on, now—what's your real name? Bill? Bob? I know you're not really a girl."

候，他们带着枪要到那儿去。"

当我听到这消息时，我的手开始颤抖起来。那女人奇怪地看着我，然后，她笑了，和蔼地说道："你说你叫什么名字？"

"玛——玛丽·威廉斯。"

"噢"，她说道，"我原以为是萨拉。"

"嗯……噢，是的，是萨拉·玛丽·威廉斯。听我说，有的人叫我萨拉，有的人叫我玛丽。"

"噢，是吗？"她又笑道，"得啦，现在把你的真实名字告诉我？比尔？鲍勃？我知道你的确不是一个女孩儿。"

strangly *adv.* 奇怪地

So then I had to tell her another story, with a different name, and I said I was running away. She said she wouldn't tell anybody, and gave me some food before I left. I hurried back to the island and Jim.

"Quick, Jim!" I cried, waking him up. "They're coming to get us!"

We got out the raft as fast as we could, put all our things on it, tied the canoe on behind, and moved off down the river. When it began to get light, we hid. When it was dark again, we travelled on. On the fifth night we passed St Louis, and we decided to go on down to Cairo in Illinois, sell the raft there and get a boat to Ohio. There are no slaves in Ohio.

We slept for most of that day and we began our *journey* again when it was dark. After some time, we saw lights on the Illinois side

---

　　然后，我不得不又编了一个谎话告诉她，谎话中我又换了一个名字，我说道，我正在离家出走。她说她不会告诉任何人，并给了我些吃的，然后我走了。我急忙回到了岛上，回到了吉姆那儿。

　　"快点，吉姆！"我喊着把他叫醒。"他们来抓我们了！"

　　我们尽快地把木筏拉出来，把我们所有的东西放在上面，把独木舟拴在木筏后面，顺流而下。天快亮时，我们藏起来。天再黑时，我们继续走。第五天夜里，我们经过了圣路易斯，我们决定继续顺流而下到伊利诺斯州的开罗去，在那儿卖掉木筏，弄条船到俄亥俄州去。俄亥俄州没有奴隶。

　　那天的大部分时间我们在睡觉，天黑时，我们又开始了我们的旅行。一段时间后，我们看到了河岸边伊利诺伊州的灯光，吉姆兴奋极了。他以

---

journey *n.* 旅行

of the river and Jim got very excited. He thought it was Cairo. Jim got the canoe ready and I went off in it to take a look at those lights. But it wasn't Cairo.

After that, we went on down the river. It was very dark that night and it wasn't easy to see where we were going. Suddenly, a big *steamboat* came at us very fast, and the next minute it was right over us. Jim and I jumped off the raft into the water. The boat hit the raft and went on up the river.

When I came up out of the water, I couldn't see Jim anywhere. I called out his name again and again, but there was no answer. "He's

---

为是开罗。吉姆把独木舟准备好,我乘着独木舟前去看看那些灯光,可那不是开罗。

之后,我们继续顺流而下。那天夜里,天很黑,不太容易看清我们在往哪儿走。突然,一艘汽船很快地冲着我们开过来了,紧接着,它朝我们头顶上压过来。我和吉姆从木筏上跳进水里。汽船撞到了木筏,继续往上游开去。

当我露出水面时,我哪儿也看不到吉姆。我一遍又一遍地大声喊着他的名字,可是没有回答。我想,"他死了!"慢慢地,我游向河边上了

---

steamboat *n.* 汽船

dead!" I thought. Slowly, I swam to the side of the river and got out. I saw that I was near a big old wooden house.

Suddenly a lot of very angry dogs jumped out at me. They made a terrible noise and someone called from the house, "Who's there?"

"George Jackson," I answered quickly. "I've fallen off a river boat."

Well, the people who lived in that house were very kind, and they took me in and gave me some new clothes and a good meal. I told them that my family were all dead, so they said I could stay with them *as long as* I wanted. It was a beautiful house and the food was good there, so I stayed.

岸。就在附近，我看到了一座宽大的老式木房子。

突然，许多发怒的狗扑向我。他们发出可怕的吠声，有人在屋里喊道，"谁在哪儿？"

"乔治·杰克逊，"我很快地回答，"我从船上掉到河里了。"

住在那房子里的人很和蔼，他们领我进屋，给了我些新衣服和一顿丰盛的饭。我告诉他们我的家人都死了，于是，他们说我想住多久就能住多久。这是一座漂亮的房子，吃得也不错，于是，我住下来了。

---

as long as 只要

A few days later one of the slaves in the house came to me and said, "Come with me!" Together, we went down to some trees by the river. "In there!" he said and went away.

On the ground, I found a man, asleep. It was Jim! I was really pleased to see him. When the steamboat hit the raft, Jim told me, the raft didn't *break up*. Jim swam after it and caught it. Then he began to look for me.

We decided to leave at once. It's all right living in a house for a little while, but you feel more free and easy and comfortable on a raft.

几天后，那家的一个奴隶来找我说，"跟我来！"我们一起来到河边的小树林。"在那儿！"他说着走开了。

我发现一个人睡在地上，是吉姆！看见他，我真是高兴极了。吉姆告诉我，汽船撞着木筏时，木筏并没有散开。吉姆游着追上那木筏并抓住了。然后，他开始寻找我。

我们决定立即离开。在房子里小住一阵还行，但在木筏上，你感到更自由、更轻松、更舒服。

---

break up　拆开；散开

Chater 4 The Duke and the King

Two or three days and nights went by and nothing much happened. We travelled at night when it was dark and everybody was asleep. We didn't want anyone to see Jim and ask questions about him.

Then, one morning, just after it was light, I found a little canoe, so I got into it and went over to the side of the river. I was looking round, when, *suddenly*, two men ran through the trees.

"Help!" they cried. "There are men and dogs trying to catch us. But we've done nothing wrong!"

第四章 公爵和国王

两三个昼夜过去了，什么事也没有发生。我们在夜里出行，那时天黑，别人都在睡觉。我们不想让任何人看见吉姆，问起有关他的问题。

一天早晨，天刚刚亮，我发现了一只小独木舟，于是，我上了独木舟来到了河边。我正在环视着，突然，两个男人跑着穿过树林。

"救命！"他们喊道。"有人想要抓我们，还带着狗。可我们没做错事！"

---

suddenly *adv.* 突然地

One of the men was about seventy years old; the other was about thirty, and they both had very old, dirty clothes. I said they could come with me, and we ran quickly back to the canoe.

Back on the raft we talked for a time and then the young man said, "My friends, I think I can tell you my secret now. I'm really a *duke*. My grandfather was the son of the Duke of Bridgewater, but he left England and came to America. When the old Duke died, my grandfather's younger brother stole everything and made himself the Duke of Bridgewater."

Well, of course, we were all very unhappy for our friend the Duke, but he said, "I'll be happier if you do things for me. Bring me my

---

其中一个人大约70岁，另外一个人大约30岁，他们俩都穿着很旧很脏的衣服。我说道，他们可以跟我来，我们很快跑回到了独木舟那儿。

回到木筏上，我们说了一会话，然后，年轻人说道，"我的朋友们，我想，现在我能告诉你们我的秘密了。其实我是个公爵。我祖父是布里奇沃特公爵的儿子，可他离开了英国，来到了美国。老公爵死时，我祖父的兄弟偷走了一切，变成了布里奇沃特公爵。"

当然了，我们为我们的公爵朋友感到很难过，但他说，"如果你们为我做事，我会更高兴。把我的饭拿来！"

---

duke *n.* 公爵

dinner!"

So we did things for him, and he liked it. But the old man spoke very little and he looked unhappy, too. After a time he said, "You know, Bridgewater, I, too, have a secret." And he began to cry.

"What do you mean?" the Duke asked. "What's your secret?"

And then the old man told us that he was really the first son of the King of France. He asked us all to go down on one knee when we spoke to him. We could call him "Your *Majesty*", too. So that was what we did, and they were both happy. Of course, I knew that they weren't really a duke and a king, but I didn't tell Jim. It's best if everybody is happy when you're living together on a raft.

所以，我们为他做事，他喜欢这样。可那个老人话说得很少，看上去也不高兴。过了一会，他说，"你要知道，布里奇沃特，我也有秘密。"他开始哭起来。

"你是什么意思？"公爵问道。"你有什么秘密？"

然后，那老人告诉我们，他的确是法国国王的长子。他要求我们跟他讲话时要单腿跪下。我们也可以称他为"陛下"。所以，这就是我们所做的一切，他们俩都很高兴。当然我知道他们根本不是什么公爵和国王，可我没告诉吉姆。当你们共同生活在一只木筏上时，如果每一个人都快乐，那是最好不过了。

---

majesty *n.* 陛下

The King and the Duke were very interested in Jim. "Is he a slave?" they wanted to know. "Is he running away?"

I had to tell them something, so I said that Jim *belonged to* my uncle and was taking me to my family in New Orleans.

"Well, we'll travel down river with you, then," said the King. "We'll have a fine time together."

So the four of us went on down the river, but Jim and I didn't like those two men. They were always getting drunk and making plans to get money out of people in every town. It's all right to take a chicken or something if you're hungry, but these men were really bad! Jim and I decided to get away from them as soon as we could. It wasn't easy because they wanted to be with us all the time.

国王和公爵对吉姆很感兴趣。"他是奴隶吗？"他们想知道，"他正在逃跑吗？"

我得对他们说些什么，于是，我说，吉姆归我叔叔所有，他正把我送到新奥尔良的家去。

"噢，那么，我们和你们一起旅行，"国王说道。"我们在一起会度过愉快的时光。"

于是，我们四人顺流而下，可我和吉姆不喜欢那两个人。他们总是喝得醉醺醺的，并计划在每一个镇上从人们那里搞到钱。如果你饿了，拿只鸡或什么的还可以，可这俩人坏透了！我和吉姆决定尽快地摆脱他们。这

---

belong to 属于

Then one morning the King went off into a town and told us to wait for him. We waited all morning and he didn't come back, so the Duke and I went into town to look for him. We looked all afternoon and in the end we found him in a bar, drunk, and then he and the Duke began to fight about some money.

"Now we can get away from them," I thought. I turned and ran back to the river. "Quick, Jim!" I shouted. "It's time to go!" But there was no answer. Jim wasn't there!

I ran into the woods, crying and shouting Jim's name. But there was still no answer.

Just then a boy came along. "Have you seen a slave?" I asked him, and I *described* Jim.

不容易，因为他们总要跟着我们。

有一天，国王到一个镇上去了，让我们等他。我们等了他一上午，他没回来，于是，我和公爵到镇上去找他。我们找了一下午，最后，在一个酒吧里找到了他，他醉醺醺的，然后，他和公爵为钱开始打起来。

"现在，我们能摆脱他们了，"我想着。我转身跑回河边。"快点，吉姆！"我大声喊着，"是走的时候了！"可没人答应。吉姆不在那儿！

我跑进树林，大声叫着吉姆的名字。可是，仍然没有回答。

正在那儿时，一个男孩过来了。"你看见一个奴隶了吗？"我问他，并描述了一下吉姆。

---

describe *v.* 描述

"Why, yes," the boy replied. "He's a *runaway* slave. I heard all about it in town. A family called the Phelpses have got him now. An old man in a bar told Mr Phelps that there was a runaway slave on a raft down by the river. He said he hadn't got time to take the slave back himself. So Mr Phelps gave him forty dollars and they went down and caught the slave this afternoon. The Phelpses are going to take him back to his owner, and they'll get three hundred dollars for him!"

I knew those two men were bad! I asked the boy where the Phelpses lived and he said it was a big white house a little way down the river.

I began to make plans to get Jim back. First, I took the raft and

---

"看见了，"那男孩回答道，"他是一个逃跑的奴隶。我是在镇上听到这些的。斐尔普斯一家人抓到了他。酒吧里的一个老头告诉斐尔普斯先生，在河下游方向河边的木筏上有一个逃跑的奴隶。他说，他自己没有时间亲自把那奴隶抓来。于是，斐尔普斯先生给了他40美元，今天下午到那去抓住了那个奴隶。斐尔普斯打算把他送回到他的主人那儿去，为了这个奴隶，他们会得到300美元！"

我知道那俩人坏透了！我问那男孩儿斐尔普斯家住哪儿，他说是河下游不太远的一座大白房子。

我开始制订救吉姆的计划。首先，我乘木筏顺流而下来到一个小岛。

---

runaway *adj.* 逃跑的

went down to a little island. I hid the raft under the trees and lay down to sleep. Before it was light, I went off down the river in the canoe. When I thought I was near the Phelpses place, I stopped, got out of the canoe and went up to the house. Suddenly, a lot of dogs ran out. They came from everywhere and they made a terrible noise.

A woman about fifty years old ran out of the house, with some little children behind her. She was smiling all over her face and she took me by the hands and cried, "It's you, at last, isn't it?"

I didn't stop to think. "Yes, *ma'am*," I said.

"Well, what took you so long? We thought you were coming two days ago. Your Uncle Silas goes to town every day to meet you. He's there now, but he'll be back soon. " She didn't stop talking and

---

我把木筏藏在树下躺下睡着了。天亮之前，我乘着独木舟顺流而下。当我觉得我已靠近斐尔普斯住处时，我停了下来，从独木舟上下来，朝那座房子走去。突然，有许多狗跑出来。他们朝我围过来发出可怕的叫声。

一位大约50岁的女人跑出屋来，身后跟着几个小孩子。她满脸笑容，拉住我的手叫道，"你终于来了，是吧？"

我连想都没想，就说，"是的，夫人，"

"是什么使你耽搁了这么久？我们以为你两天前就到那。你的姨夫赛拉斯每天都到镇上去接你。他现在就在那儿，不过，他很快就会回来。"她不停地说着，我无法告诉她，是她弄错了。"把他们的事都告诉我，"

---

ma'am *n.* 夫人；女士

I couldn't tell her that she was making a mistake. "Tell us all about them," she cried. "Tell me everything."

I knew then that I had to tell her... but just then she cried, "Here he is! Quick, hide!" and she *pushed* me inside the house and behind the front door. Then her husband came in and she asked him, "Has he come?"

"No," her husband replied.

"Look!" she shouted, and then she pulled me out from behind the door.

"Why, who's that?" Mr Phelps cried, surprised.

"It's Tom Sawyer!" she laughed.

她大声说道。"把一切都告诉我。"

那时我明白了，我不得不告诉她……可就在那时，她喊道，"他来了！快点，藏起来！"她把我推到屋里，藏在前门后。然后，她丈夫走了进来，她问他，"他来了吗？"

"没有，"她丈夫回答道。

"看看！"她大声说道，然后，她把我从门后拉出来。

"咦，这是谁？"斐尔普斯先生惊奇地大声说道。

"这是汤姆·索亚！"她笑道。

---

push *v.* 推

Chater 5 The Plan to Free Jim

When I heard that, I *nearly* fell through the floor, but it was a big piece of luck. It was easy for me to be Tom Sawyer because Tom was my best friend. He and his brother Sid lived with their Aunt Polly up in St Petersburg, and I knew all about them. Now I learnt that Aunt Polly had a sister, who was Mrs Phelps. She and her husband were Tom's Aunt Sally and Uncle Silas. And Tom was coming down south by boat to stay with them for a bit.

We all sat there talking and I could answer all their questions about the Sawyer family. I was feeling really happy about this when

第五章 使吉姆获得自由的计划

当我听到这话时，我差点儿没掉进地板缝里去，不过，这可是太幸运了。冒充汤姆·索亚对我来说是件容易事，因为，汤姆是我最好的朋友。他和他的弟弟锡德和他们的波莉姨妈一起住在圣彼得斯堡，他们的事我都知道。现在，我知道了波莉姨妈有一个妹妹，她是斐尔普斯太太。她和她的丈夫是汤姆的萨莉姨妈和赛拉斯姨夫。汤姆要乘船南下和他们小住一阵。

我们都坐在那儿聊着天，我可以回答所有的有关索亚家的问题。对此

nearly *adv.* 几乎

suddenly I heard a boat on the river. "Tom could be on that boat," I thought, "and he's going to walk in here and call out my name before I can stop him. I've got to go and meet him."

So I told the Phelpses that I would go into town to get my bags, which were at the boat station. I hurried up the road and before I was *halfway* to town, there was Tom Sawyer coming along.

When he saw me, his mouth fell open and he looked a bit white in the face. "Aren't you dead?" he said. "Everybody said that you were murdered!"

"I'm not dead yet," I said, "but listen…" I told him about my adventures, and Tom loved all that. Then I told him about the

---

我感到很高兴。突然，我听到河上的船声。"汤姆可能在那条船上，"我想着，"他会走进这屋里来，我还来不及阻止他，他就会大声喊出我的名字。我得去迎他。"

于是，我告诉斐尔普斯一家，我要到镇子上的船站去取我的包。我急忙上路，还没走出一半路远，汤姆·索亚沿路走来了。

他看见我时，嘴张着，脸色略微发白，"难道你没死？"他说道。"大家都说，你被杀死了！"

"我还没死呢，"我说道，"可你听着……"我对他讲了我的冒险，汤姆非常喜爱这一切。然后，我跟他讲了斐尔普斯一家的事，并告诉他，

---

halfway *adj.* 半途的

Phelpses and that they thought I was Tom Sawyer. "What shall we do?" I asked him.

Tom thought for a bit, and then he said, "I know. You take my bags and say they're yours. I'll come to the house in about half an hour."

"All right," I said, "but there's another thing. You know old Miss Watson's slave Jim, who ran away? Well, he's a *prisoner* here, and I'm going to help him escape."

"Jim?" Tom said. "But he's—" Then he stopped and thought. "Right. I'll help, too, I'll make a really good plan." He looked very excited.

他们以为我是汤姆·索亚。"我们该怎么办呢？"我问他。

汤姆略加思索，然后说道，"我知道怎么办。你把我的包拿去，就说是你的。我大约半小时后到。"

"好吧，"我说，"可还有一件事。你知道老沃森小姐的奴隶吉姆吗？他逃走了。唉，他是这儿的一个囚犯，我打算帮助他逃走。"

"吉姆？"汤姆说道。"可他是——"然后，他停下来思考了一下。"好吧，我也帮忙，我要制订一个很好的计划。"他看起来很兴奋。

---

prisoner *n.* 囚犯

So I went back to the house with the bags, and Tom came along half an hour later. He knocked on the door and when his Aunt Sally opened it, he said he was Sid, Tom's brother. He wanted his visit to be a surprise for his dear old Aunt Sally, he said.

Well, Aunt Sally was very pleased to see Tom and Sid. She thought it was wonderful. She and Uncle Silas were really nice people.

When we were alone later, Tom and I talked about Jim's escape. I said I had a plan, and Tom listened to it.

"It's a good plan," he said when I finished. "But it's too easy! It's got to be a real escape, like a real adventure in a story book. So we want something difficult and *dangerous*. Now, listen to this…"

于是，我拿着包回去了，汤姆半小时后来了。他敲了敲门，萨莉姨妈开门时，他说，他是锡德，汤姆的弟弟。他想使他的来访给他那亲爱的萨莉姨妈一个惊喜，他说道。

嘿，萨莉姨妈看见汤姆和锡德真是高兴极了。她觉得这真是太好了。她和赛拉斯姨夫的确是很好的人。

我们俩单独在一起时，我和汤姆谈起了吉姆逃跑的事。我说，我有一个计划，汤姆听着我的计划。

"这是一个好计划，"我讲完后他说道。"可太容易了！得像个真正的逃跑，像故事书中的真正的冒险。所以，我们要让这冒险困难点，危险

---

dangerous *adj.* 危险的

So he told me his plan. I knew it would be a good one because Tom's plans are always crazy and exciting.

And we sure had a lot of fun with that plan! We knew that Jim was locked up in a *hut* outside the house. Every night we got out through our bedroom window and dug a hole right under the wall of the hut. It took us a week, and it was hard work. We talked to Jim secretly and told him about the plan, and he was really pleased.

We also wrote secret letters to everybody. Tom said that people always do this in books. We wrote that there was a gang of slave-thieves coming up from the south. They wanted to steal Jim and get the three hundred dollars from his owner. Well, the Phelpses and

点。听听这个……"

于是，他告诉了我他的计划。我明白，这会是一个出色的计划，因为，汤姆的计划总是既疯狂又兴奋。

执行那计划肯定会给我们带来许多的乐趣！我们知道，吉姆被锁在屋外的一个小屋里。每天夜里，我们都从卧室的窗户钻出去，就在小屋墙下挖洞。挖洞花费了我们一星期的时间，这是一件苦差事。我们秘密地同吉姆交谈，并告诉他我们的计划，他高兴极了。

我们也给大家写密信。汤姆说，书中人们总是这样做。我们写道，有一群盗奴贼从南方来。他们想偷走吉姆，从他的主人那儿得到300美元。

hut *n.* 小屋

their friends got very excited, and on the night of the escape I went into the sitting-room, and there was *a crowd of* men in there—all with guns!

I ran and told Tom, and he said that this was really good. "It's a real adventure now, all right, " he said, very excited. "Perhaps they'll come after us, and shoot, and we'll all get killed!"

Well, there wasn't time to think about it because it all happened so quickly. We got Jim out through the hole under the wall, and began to run down to the river. But the men heard us and came after us. They began to shoot, and so we ran as fast as we could to the canoe. We got in it and went over to Spanish Island. My raft was

---

斐尔普斯一家和他们的朋友很兴奋，逃跑的那天夜里，我走进起居室，那儿有一大群男人——都拿着枪！

我跑去告诉了汤姆，他说这真不错。"好吧，这是一次真正的冒险，"他说道，很兴奋。"或许他们会追我们，开枪，我们都会被打死！"

没有时间考虑了，因为，这一切发生得太快了。我们把吉姆从墙下的洞里弄出来。开始往河边跑去。但是，那些人听到了我们的声音，追了过来，他们开始开枪，我们尽快地往独木舟那儿跑去。我们上了独木舟，前往西班牙岛。我的木筏停在那儿，我们的计划就是逃到那岛上，然后继续

---

a crowd of   一群

there, and our plan was to escape on that and go on down river.

"Now, Jim," I cried, "you're a free man! " We were all very happy, but Tom was the happiest of all, because he had a *bullet* in his leg.

When Jim and I heard that, we weren't so happy. Tom wanted the adventure to go on, but Jim and I said that a doctor must look at Tom's leg. Tom was getting angry about this, but Jim said:

"You listen to me, Tom Sawyer. You say I'm a free man now, and perhaps I am. But old Jim is not going to run away and leave one of his friends with a bullet in his leg! So I'm staying right here until a doctor comes."

顺流而下。

"嗨，吉姆，"我喊道，"你是一个自由之人了！"我们都很高兴，可汤姆是最高兴的一个，因为，他腿上中了一枪。

我和吉姆听到这话时，可不那么高兴了。汤姆想让这冒险继续下去，可我和吉姆说，一定要找个医生看看汤姆的腿。汤姆对此生气了，可吉姆说道：

"你听我说，汤姆·索亚。你说，我现在是一个自由人了，或许我是。可老吉姆不会逃跑，而丢下一个腿里有颗子弹的朋友！所以，我就待在这儿，一直到医生来。"

---

bullet *n.* 子弹

I knew Jim would say that. He was a good, true friend, and you can't say that about many people.

Well, that was the end of the adventure, really. I went and found a doctor in the town. He was a kind old man, and he said he would go over to the island. But Tom's leg got very bad, and the next day the doctor and some other men carried Tom to the Phelpses' house. They brought Jim too, and they *locked* him *up* in the hut again. But the doctor said, "Be kind to him, because he didn't run away and he stayed to help me with the boy."

They took Tom up to bed because his leg was really bad, and Aunt Sally sat with him while he slept. I didn't want to answer any questions so I kept out of everybody's way.

　　我知道，吉姆会这样说的。他是一个真正的好朋友，对许多其他的人，你不会这样说的。

　　说真的，这就是冒险的结束。我去到镇上找了个医生。他是个和蔼的老人，他说，他会到岛上去。可汤姆腿的伤势很重，第二天，医生和其他的一些人把汤姆抬到斐尔普斯家。他们也带回了吉姆，他们又把他锁在木屋里。可医生说，"对他好点儿，因为他没逃跑，他留在那儿帮我照顾这个男孩。"

　　他们把汤姆放在床上，因为，他腿的伤势很重，他睡觉时，萨莉姨妈坐在他的身边。我不想回答任何问题，所以，我远远地躲开大家。

---

lock up　将……锁住

When Tom woke up the next day, he felt better. I was in the room and he said to me, "Jim's all right, isn't he?"

I didn't know what to say because Aunt Sally was listening, and before I could stop him, Tom went on:

"We did it, Aunt Sally. Me and Tom here. We helped Jim escape." He told her all about the *digging* and everything, and Aunt Sally's mouth was opening and closing like a fish. Then she got really angry with Tom.

"That slave is locked up again and he's going to stay there. And if I catch you again—"

Tom suddenly sat up in bed. "You can't do that!" he cried. "Jim

第二天，汤姆醒来时，他感觉好多了。我在他房间里，他对我说，"吉姆没事儿，是吧？"

我不知道说什么好，因为萨莉姨妈在听着，我还来不及阻止他，汤姆继续说道：

"这件事是我们干的，萨莉姨妈。是我和汤姆。我们帮助吉姆逃跑的。"他把挖洞和所有的一切都告诉了她，萨莉姨妈的嘴像条鱼一样一张一闭。然后，她真的生汤姆的气了。

"那个奴隶又被锁了起来，他要待在那儿。如果我再抓到你——"

汤姆突然在床上坐起来。"你不能那样做！"他喊道。"吉姆是老沃

dig *v.* 挖掘

was old Miss Watson's slave, but she died two months ago. Before she died, she wrote that she wanted Jim to be free, and not a slave any more. Jim's a free man, not a slave!"

Well, that was a surprise to me and Aunt Sally! She thought Tom was crazy. "But Sid, why did you help him to escape, if he was free already?" she said.

"I wanted the adventure, of course!" said Tom. "We made a really exciting plan and...Oh my! ...AUNT POLLY!"

We turned round, and there was Tom's Aunt Polly in the *doorway*! That was the second big surprise. Aunt Sally was really pleased to see her sister, and jumped up to put her arms round her. I got under

---

森小姐的奴隶，可她两个月前去世了。死前她写道，她要让吉姆自由，不再是一个奴隶了。吉姆是一个自由人，不再是一个奴隶！"

我和萨莉姨妈都感到很惊讶！她觉得汤姆疯了。"可是，锡德，如果他已经自由了，那你为什么还帮他逃跑呢？"她说道。

"当然，我想冒险！"汤姆说。"我们制订了一个很令人兴奋的计划，并且……呀，天哪！……波莉姨妈！"

我们转过身来，汤姆的波莉姨妈站在门那儿！这是第二个令人大吃一惊的事。萨莉姨妈见到她的姐姐的确很高兴，跳起来搂住了她。我赶快爬

---

doorway *n.* 门口

the bed as fast as I could. There was trouble coming for me and Tom, that was for sure.

Then Aunt Polly said to Tom, "You always were a terrible boy, Tom Sawyer, and I want to know—"

"But Polly dear," said Aunt Sally, "this isn't Tom. It's Sid. Tom was here a minute ago. Where is he?"

"Where's Huck Finn, you mean," replied Aunt Polly. "Come out from under that bed, Huck Finn."

So Tom and I had to *explain* everything. Aunt Polly said that Aunt Sally wrote and told her that Tom and Sid were there. She knew

到床底下。我和汤姆要有麻烦了，这是确定无疑的。

然后，波莉姨妈对汤姆说道，"你总是捣乱，汤姆·索亚，我想知道——"

"可是，亲爱的波莉，"萨莉姨妈说道，"这不是汤姆，是锡德。汤姆刚才还在这呢。他哪儿去了？"

"你是指哈克·费恩哪儿去了？"波莉姨妈回答道，"从床底下出来，哈克·费恩。"

所以，我和汤姆不得不解释所有这一切。波莉姨妈说，萨莉姨妈写信

explain v. 解释

that it wasn't true, so she *decided to* come and find out what was happening. But she said that it was true about Miss Watson and that Jim was a free man now.

We got Jim out of the hut and Aunt Sally and Uncle Silas were really nice to him. Later, Tom, Jim and I had a long talk by ourselves. Tom talked and talked, and then he said, "Let's all three of us run away one night, and go and have adventures in the wild country down south."

It sounded like a good plan to me. "The only thing is," I said, "I haven't got any money to buy the right clothes and things. All my money back in St Petersburg will be in Pop's pockets by now."

告诉她，汤姆和锡德在那儿。她知道这不是真的，于是，她决定来弄清楚到底是怎么回事。可她说，沃森小姐的事倒是真的，吉姆现在是一个自由人了。

我们把吉姆从小屋里放出来，萨莉姨妈和赛拉斯姨夫对他很友好。后来，汤姆、吉姆和我，就我们三个人，聊了很长时间。汤姆不停地说着，然后，他说道，"有那么一天夜里，我们三个人逃走，到南方荒野的地方去冒险。"

听起来倒是一个不错的计划。"唯一的事情是，"我说道；"我没有钱买合适的衣服和物品。我所有的在圣彼得斯堡的钱这时应该在爸爸的兜

---

decide to 决定

"No," said Tom. "Your money's all there. Your Pop never came back."

"No, and he won't come back, Huck," Jim said. "You remember that dead man on the river, when I said 'Don't look at his face'? Well, that was your Pop. You can get your money when you want."

Tom's leg is almost better now, and I haven't got any more to write about. I'm really pleased about that because it was very difficult to write a book and I won't do it again. But I think I'm going to have to *run away* before the others, because Aunt Sally wants me to live with her. I'll have to sleep in a bed and wear clean clothes and learn to be good, and I can't do that again. I've done it once already.

里了。"

"不会的，"汤姆说道。"你的钱都在那儿。你爸爸从来没回来。"

"对了，他不会回来了，哈克，"吉姆说道。"你记得河上那个死人吗？我说'别看他的脸'，那就是你爸爸。你想拿到钱时，你就能拿到。"

汤姆的腿现在差不多好了，我没有什么要写的了。对此我很高兴，因为，写一本书很难，我不会再写了。可我想，在其他人逃跑之前，我得准备先逃走，因为萨莉姨妈想让我和她住在一起。我将不得不睡在床上，穿干净衣服，学着有教养，我不能再那样了。我已经尝试过一次了。

run away 逃跑

03

Robinson Crusoe

Chater 1 My First Sea Journey

Before I begin my story, I would like to tell you a little about myself.

I was born in the year 1632, in the city of York in the north of England. My father was German, but he came to live and work in England. Soon after that, he *married* my mother, who was English. Her family name was Robinson, so, when I was born, they called me Robinson, after her.

鲁宾孙漂流记

第一章 我的第一次海上旅行

开始我的故事之前，我想先向你谈一点我自己的情况。

我1632年出生在英国北部的约克郡。我父亲是德国人，但他却来到英国居住和工作。此后不久，他与我母亲结了婚，我母亲是英国人。娘家姓鲁宾孙，因此，我出生后他们都称呼我鲁宾孙，沿用了我母亲的姓氏。

---

marry *v.* 结婚

My father did well in his business and I went to a good school. He wanted me to get a good job and live a quiet, comfortable life. But I didn't want that. I wanted adventure and an exciting life.

"I want to be a *sailor* and go to sea," I told my mother and father. They were very unhappy about this.

"Please don't go," my father said. "You won't be happy, you know. Sailors have a difficult and dangerous life." And because I loved him, and he was unhappy, I tried to forget about the sea.

But I couldn't forget, and about a year later, I saw a friend in town. His father had a ship, and my friend said to me, "We're sailing to London tomorrow. Why don't you come with us?"

And so, on September 1st, 1651, I went to Hull, and the next day we sailed for London.

　　我父亲在生意上做得很出色，并且我也进了一所好学校。他希望我得到好的工作，过一种平静的、舒适的生活。但是我不希望如此。我喜欢冒险和刺激的生活。

　　"我想成为一名水手去航行，"我告诉父母亲。他们对此很不高兴。

　　"不要去，"父亲说。"你不会幸福的，你知道。水手过着艰苦而且危险的生活。"因为我爱父亲，他不高兴，我便试图忘掉大海。

　　但我不可能忘掉，大约一年后，我在镇里遇到一个朋友。他的父亲有一艘船，我的朋友对我说，"明天我们航行去伦敦。你为什么不和我们一起走呢？"

　　于是，1651年9月1日，我到了赫尔港，第二天我们驶向伦敦。

---

sailor *n.* 水手

But, a few days later, there was a strong wind. The sea was *rough* and dangerous, and the ship went up and down, up and down. I was very ill, and very afraid.

"Oh, I don't want to die!" I cried. "I want to live! If I live, I'll go home and never go to sea again!"

The next day the wind dropped, and the sea was quiet and beautiful again.

"Well, Bob," my friend laughed. "How do you feel now? The wind wasn't too bad."

"What!" I cried. "It was a terrible storm."

"Oh, that wasn't a storm," my friend answered. "Just a little wind. Forget it. Come and have a drink."

但是，几天后，刮起了狂风。狂暴的大海危机四伏，船不断颠簸。我晕船晕得厉害，非常害怕。

"噢，我不想死！"我哭喊起来。"我想活着！假如我活着，我就要回家，再也不出海了！"

第二天，风停了，大海又重新恢复了平静而美丽。

"好了，鲍伯，"我的朋友笑着说。"现在你感觉如何？这风并不太令人讨厌。"

"什么！"我大叫起来。"这可是一场可怕的风暴。"

"噢，这不算风暴，"我的朋友回答。"仅仅是小风而已。忘记它

---

rough *adj.* 粗暴的

After a few drinks with my friend, I felt better. I forgot about the danger and decided not to go home. I didn't want my friends and family to laugh at me! I stayed in London for some time, but I still wanted to go to sea. So, when the *captain* of a ship asked me to go with him to Guinea in Africa, I agreed. And so I went to sea for the second time.

It was a good ship and everything went well at first, but I was very ill again.

Then, when we were near the Canary Islands, a Turkish pirate ship came after us.

吧，来，喝一杯。"

和朋友喝了几杯，我感觉好多了。我忘记了危险，决定不回家了。我不愿意我的朋友和家人嘲笑我！我在伦敦停留了一段时间，但我仍然想去航行。所以，当一位船长要求我和他一起去非洲的几内亚时，我答应了。于是，我第二次去航海。

这是一艘好船，开始一切都很顺利，但是我又晕得厉害。

此后，当我们接近加纳利群岛时，一艘土耳其海盗船跟上了我们。

---

captain *n.* 船长

They were famous thieves of the sea at that time. There was a long, hard fight, but when it finished, we and the ship were prisoners.

The Turkish captain and his men took us to Sallee in Morocco. They wanted to sell us as slaves in the markets there. But in the end the Turkish captain decided to keep me for himself, and took me home with him. This was a sudden and terrible change in my life. I was now a slave and this Turkish captain was my *master*.

他们是当时有名的海盗。经过一场长时间激烈的交火一切都结束时，我们连人带船都成了俘虏。

土耳其船长和他的部下把我们带到摩洛哥的萨利。他们想在那儿的市场上把我们当做奴隶卖掉。但最后土耳其船长决定把我留给他自己，带我随他回家。这是我一生中一次突然的可怕变故。现在我成了奴隶，这位土耳其船长是我的主人。

---

master *n.* 主人

Chater 2 Down the Coast of Africa

For two long years I lived the life of a slave. I worked in the house, the garden, everyday I plan to escape, but it was never *possible*. I thought about it day and night. My master liked to go fishing in a little boat, and he always took me with him. A man called Moely, and a young boy also went with us.

One day my master said to us, "Some of my friends want to go fishing tomorrow. Get the boat ready."

So we put a lot of food and drink on the boat, and the next morning, we waited for my master and his friends. But when my master arrived, he was alone.

第二章 南下非洲海岸

两年多的时间里，我过着奴隶的生活。我在屋子里、花园里干活，每天都计划着逃跑，但一直没能成功。我日夜思考着逃跑的事。我的主人喜欢乘小船去钓鱼，而且总是带上我。一个名叫莫雷的男人及一个小男孩也总跟随着我们。

一天主人对我们说："我有些朋友明天想去钓鱼。把船给准备好。"

于是，我们搬了很多食物和饮料到船上，在第二天早上，我们等候着主人和他的朋友。但主人来时却是他独自一人。

possible *adj.* 可能的

"My friends don't want to go fishing today," he said to me. "But you go with Moely and the boy, and catch some fish for our supper tonight."

"Yes, master," I answered quietly, but inside I was excited. "Perhaps now I can escape," I said to myself.

My master went back to his friends and we took the boat out to sea. For a time we fished quietly, and then I moved carefully behind Moely and knocked him into the water.

"Swim!" I cried. "Swim to the shore!"

My master liked to shoot *seabirds* and so there were guns on the boat. Quickly, I took one of these guns. Moely was swimming after the boat and I shouted to him:

"我的朋友今天不想去钓鱼了，"他对我说，"但你和莫雷及这孩子去为我们今天的晚餐捕些鱼来。"

"是，主人。"我平静地回答，但我内心很激动。心想，"也许这回我可以逃脱了。"

主人回到他的朋友们那儿去了，我们坐船出了海。静静地钓了一阵鱼，然后我小心翼翼地移到莫雷的身后把他推到了海里。

"游回去！"我大声喊着"朝岸上游！"

我的主人喜欢打海鸟，所以有几支枪在船上。我迅速地抓过一支枪，莫雷正跟在船后面游，我朝他叫道：

---

seabird *n.* 海鸟

"Go back to the *shore*! You can swim there—it's not too far. I won't hurt you, but if you come near the boat, I'll shoot you through the head!" So Moely turned, and swam back to the shore as quickly as he could.

Then I said to the boy, "Xury, if you help me, I'll be a good friend to you. If you don't help me, I'll push you into the sea too."

But Xury was happy to help me. "I'll go all over the world with you," he cried.

I wanted to sail to the Canary Islands, but I was afraid to go too far from the shore. It was only a small boat. And so we sailed on south for some days. We had very little water, and it was dangerous

---

"回到岸上去！你可以游到那儿，这儿离海岸不太远。我不会伤害你，但如果你一靠近这只船，我就会打穿你的脑袋！"于是，莫雷转过身以最快的速度游回岸上去了。

然后，我对这小孩说："苏里，如果你帮我，我会是你的好朋友。如果你不帮我，我同样会把你丢到海里去。"

但苏里很乐意帮助我。"我愿意跟着你走遍世界，"他大声说。

我想驶向加纳利群岛，但是不敢远离海岸，这只是一艘小船。因此我们向南航行了几天，我们只有很少的水，这儿是危险的国度，有许多野生动物。我们害怕，但是我们常常不得不上岸去取水。有一次我用枪射死了

---

shore n. 岸

country here, with many wild animals. We were afraid, but we often had to go on shore to get more water. Once I used a gun to shoot a wild animal. I don't know what animal it was, but it made a good meal.

For about ten or twelve days we sailed on south, down the *coast* of Africa. Then one day we saw some people on the shore—strange, wild people, who did not look friendly. By now we had very little food, and We really needed help. we were afraid, but we had to go on shore.

At first, they were afraid of us, too. Perhaps white people never visited this coast. We did not speak their language, of course, so we

---

一只野兽，我不知道这是什么动物，但它成了一顿美餐。

沿着非洲海岸我们朝南航行了大约10天至12天。随后一天我们看到岸上有些人——古怪的野人，他们看起来并不友善，那时我们的食物很少了，我们实在需要帮助，我们害怕，但我们不得不上岸。

开始，他们也害怕我们。或许白人从没有访问过这海岸。当然，我们不会说他们的语言，我们只好用手势和脸部表情来表明我们很饿。他们把食物搬给我们，随即迅速地离开。我们把食物搬上船，他们看着我们。我

---

coast *n.* 海岸

used our hands and faces to show that we were hungry. They came with food for us, but then they moved away quickly. We carried the food to our boat, and they watched us. I tried to thank them, but I had nothing to give them.

Just then two big wild cats came down to the shore from the mountains. I think they were *leopards*. The people were afraid of these wild cats, and the women cried out. Quickly, I took a gun, and shot one of the animals. The second wild cat ran back up into the mountains.

Guns were new to these African people, and they were afraid of the loud noise and the smoke. But they were happy about the dead

试图感谢他们，却没有什么东西可以送给他们。

正在这时候，两只大野猫从山上窜到海边来。我想它们是豹子。那些人害怕这些野猫，那些妇女们尖叫起来。很快地，我拿起一支枪，击中了其中一只野兽。另外一只跑回了山里。

枪对这些非洲居民来说很新奇，他们害怕这轰响的声音与烟雾。但他们对死的野猫很感兴趣。我送给他们这只死兽的肉，他们给了我们更多的

leopard *n.* 豹

wild cat. I gave them the meat of the dead animal, and they gave us more food and water.

We now had a lot of food and water, and we *sailed* on. Eleven days later we came near the Cape Verde Islands. We could see them, but we couldn't get near because there was no wind. We waited.

Suddenly Xury called to me, "Look, a ship!"

He was right! We called and shouted and sailed our little boat as fast as we could. But the ship did not see us. Then I remembered the guns which made a lot of smoke. A few minutes later the ship saw us and turned.

食物和水。

现在我们有了很多的食物和水，我们继续航行。11天后我们接近佛得角群岛。我们可以看见它们，但由于没有风我们不能靠近。我们等候着。

突然，苏里对我叫着，"看哪，一只船！"

他是对的！我们叫喊着并且尽可能快地划着小船。但是那只船并没看到我们。这时我想起枪可以产生很多烟雾。几分钟后那只船看到了我们并且转了过来。

sail *v.* 航行

When we were on the ship, the Portuguese captain listened to my story. He was going to Brazil and agreed to help me, but he wanted nothing for his help. "No," he said, when I tried to pay him. "Perhaps, one day, someone will help me when I need it."

But he gave me money for my boat, and for Xury, too. At first, I did not want to sell Xury as a slave, after all our dangerous adventures together. But Xury was happy to go to the captain, and the captain was a good man. "In ten years' time," he said, "Xury can go free."

When we arrived in Brazil three weeks later, I *said goodbye to* the captain and Xury, left the ship, and went to begin a new life.

等我们上了他们的船，葡萄牙船长倾听了我的故事。他正要去巴西并且答应帮助我，但他对我的帮助不要任何回报。当我试图付钱给他时，他说："不，也许，有一天，当我需要帮助时，有人也会帮助我。"

但是他却付钱买下我的船，也买下了苏里。起初，我不愿意把苏里卖作奴隶，毕竟一起经历了我们所有危险的冒险过程。但苏里很乐意跟随船长，这位船长是一个好人。"十年后，"他说，"苏里将会获得自由。"

三星期后我们抵达巴西，我告别了船长和苏里，离开了船，继续开始了一个新的生活。

---

say goodbye to　向……告别

Chater 3 The Storm and the Shipwreck

I stayed in Brazil and worked hard for some years. By then I was rich...but also bored.

One day some friends came to me and said, "We're going to Africa to do business. Why don't you come with us? We'll all be rich after this journey!"

How stupid I was! I had an easy, comfortable life in Brazil, but, of course, I agreed. And so, in 1659, I *went to sea* again.

At first, all went well, but then there was a terrible storm. For twelve days the wind and the rain didn't stop. We lost three men in the sea,

---

第三章 风暴与海难

我留在巴西苦干了几年。不久我就有了一笔财富……但我又感到了厌倦。

一天，一些朋友来看我并对我说，"我们将要去非洲做生意。为什么你不和我们一起去呢？这次航行后我们都会发财的！"

我是多么傻啊！我在巴西已有了轻松、舒适的生活，然而我又同意了。于是，在1659年，我又一次出海了。

最初，一帆风顺，但不久就来了一场可怕的风暴。狂风暴雨持续了12天没有停息。我们在海上失去了三个同伴，而且没多久，船舷上就出现

---

go to sea   出海

and soon the ship had holes in its sides. "We're all going to die this time," I said to myself. Then one morning one of the *sailors* saw land, but the next minute our ship hit some sand just under the sea. The ship could not move and we were really in danger now. The sea was trying to break the ship into pieces, and we had very little time. Quickly, we put a boat into the sea and got off the ship. But the sea was very rough and our little boat could not live for long in that wild water.

Half an hour later the angry sea turned our boat over and we were all in the water. I looked round for my friends, but I could see nobody. I was alone.

That day I was lucky, and the sea carried me to the shore. I could not see the land, only mountains of water all around me. Then,

---

了漏洞。"这回我们都活不成了，"我自言自语。一天早上，一个水手看见了陆地，但紧接着我们的船就触到了海底的沙滩。船没法移动，我们此刻真正地陷入了危险之中。海浪似乎极力地想把船击成粉碎，我们只有很少的时间了。迅速地，我们把小艇放到海里，离开了船。但大海太粗暴了我们的小船在这样的大浪中根本没法长时间航行。

半个时辰后，愤怒的大海掀翻了我们的小船，我们全都落到了水里。我四处张望寻视我的伙伴，但却看不到一个人。只剩我一人了。

那天，我是幸运的，海水把我送到了岸边。我没法看见陆地，我的四周只有排山倒海的浪涛。突然间我触到了脚下的陆地。又一个浪峰盖过

---

sailor *n.* 水手

suddenly, I felt the ground under my feet. Another mountain of water came, pushed me up the beach, and I fell on the wet sand.

At first I was very thankful to be alive. Slowly, I got to my feet and went higher up the shore. From there, I looked out to sea. I could see our ship, but it was *wrecked* and there was nobody near it. There was nobody in the water. All my friends were dead. I was alive, but in a strange wild country, with no food, no water, and no gun.

It was dark now and I was tired. I was afraid to sleep on the shore. Perhaps there were wild animals there. So I went up into a tree and I stayed there all night.

来，把我推上了沙滩，我跌倒在湿湿的沙地上。

最初，我非常庆幸我还活着。慢慢地我站起来，走到高处的岸上。在那儿，我眺望大海。我能够看见我们的船，但它已倾覆了。船的附近没有一个人，水中也没有人。我的伙伴们都死了。我活着，但却在一个陌生的荒山野地，没有食物，没有水，没有枪支。

此刻，天黑了，我很累。我不敢睡在岸上，也许这儿有野兽，我只好爬到一棵树上过了一夜。

---

wreck *v.* 使（船舶）失事；使下沉

Chater 4 A New Life on an Island

When day came, the sea was quiet again. I looked for our ship and, *to my surprise*, it was still there and still in one piece. "I think I can swim to it," I said to myself. So I walked down to the sea and before long, I was at the ship and was swimming round it.

But how could I get on to it? In the end, I got in through a hole in the side, but it wasn't easy.

There was a lot of water in the ship, but the sand under the sea was still holding the ship in one place. The back of the ship was high out of the water, and I was very thankful for this because all the ship's food was there. I was very hungry so I began to eat something

第四章 孤岛上的新生活

当白天到来时，大海又恢复了平静。我找我们的船，令我惊诧的是它依然在那儿并且没有破碎。"我想我能够游到那儿，"我自言自语。于是，我朝大海里走去，不一会儿，我靠近了船绕着它游。

只是，我怎样才可以上去呢？最后，我从船舷一侧的一个洞里钻了进去，但却很不容易。

船里积了很多水，但海底的沙使船固定在了一个地方。船的尾部翘出了水面，这让我非常庆幸，因为船上全部的食物都储在那儿。我已经很饿，所以我马上开始吃东西。然后决定带一些食物回到岸上。可是我又怎

to one's surprise　　使某人惊讶的是

at once. Then I decided to take some of it back to the shore with me. But how could I get it there?

I looked around the ship, and after a few minutes, I found some long pieces of wood. I tied them together with rope. Then I got the things that I wanted from the ship. There was a big box of food— rice, and salted meat, and hard ship's bread. I also took many strong knives and other tools, the ship's sails and ropes, paper, pens, books, and seven guns. Now I needed a little sail from the ship, and then I was ready. Slowly and carefully, I went back to the shore. It was difficult to stop my things from falling into the sea, but in the end I got everything on to the shore.

样才能做到呢?

我察看了这只船的四周，几分钟后，我找到了几块长条的木板。我用绳子把它们紧扎在一起。然后我便搬上我想从船上带走的东西。那儿有一大箱食品——米、咸肉和硬面包。我还拿了很多坚固的小刀及其他工具，船帆、绳子、纸、钢笔、书及7支枪。现在我需要在船上找一个小帆，不一会儿，我就找好了。我慢慢地、小心翼翼地向岸边划，要使我的东西不掉到海里是挺困难的，但最终我把每一件东西都弄上了岸。

---

at once 立刻

Now I needed somewhere to keep my things.

There were some hills around me, so I decided to build myself a little house on one of them. I walked to the top of the highest hill and looked down, I was very unhappy, because I saw then that I was on an island. There were two smaller islands a few miles away, and after that, only the sea. Just the sea, for mile after mile.

After a time, I found a little cave in the side of a hill. In front of it, there was a good place to make a home. So, I used the ship's sails, rope, and pieces of wood, and after a lot of hard work I had a very fine *tent*. The cave at the back of my tent was a good place to keep my food, and so I called it my "kitchen". That night, I went to sleep in my new home.

The next day I thought about the possible dangers on the isand.

现在，我需要地方来存放我的东西。

在我的周围有些小山丘，于是我决定在其中的一个小山上给自己建一座小屋。我走到最高的小山山顶往下看，我非常沮丧，因为那时我才明白我是在一个孤岛上。几英里外有两个更小的岛，更远的地方，只剩下了大海，延绵数英里的大海。

过了不久，我在小山的一侧找到了一个小洞穴。在它前面，是一个安家的好地方。于是，我用那些船的帆，绳子及木板经过很艰苦的劳作，我有了一个非常好的帐篷。帐篷后面的洞穴是存放食物的好地方，所以我称之为我的"厨房"。那天晚上，我便在我的新家睡觉。

第二天，我仔细设想了岛上可能存在的危险。在我的岛上，会不会有

tent *n.* 帐篷

Were there wild animals, and perhaps wild people too, on my island? I didn't know, but I was very afraid. So I decided to build a very strong fence. I cut down young trees and put them in the ground, in a half circle around the front of my tent. I used many of the ship's *ropes* too, and in the end my fence was as strong as a stone wall. Nobody could get over it, through it, or round it.

Making tents and building fences is hard work. I needed many tools to help me. So I decided to go back to the ship again, and get some more things. I went back twelve times, but soon after my twelfth visit there was another terrible storm. The next morning, when I looked out to sea, there was no ship.

野兽，也许还会存在野人？虽然我不知道，但却很害怕。于是我决定建一个坚固的栅栏。我砍倒了一些小树插入到地上在我的帐篷前围成个半圆。我还用了很多船上的绳子，最后我的栅栏就像一堵坚固的石墙。没有人可以翻进来，钻进来或者绕过来。

制作帐篷和建造栅栏篱笆是一项艰苦的工作。我需要很多工具来帮我。所以，我打算再次回到船上，去拿更多的东西。我回去了12次，但就在我第12次回来之后不久又来了一场暴风雨。第二天一早我朝外瞧向大海时，船不见了。

rope *n.* 绳子

When I saw that, I was very unhappy. "Why am I alive, and why are all my friends dead?" I asked myself. "What will happen to me now, alone on this island without friends? How can I ever escape from it?"

Then I told myself that I was lucky—lucky to be alive, lucky to have food and tools, lucky to be young and strong. But I knew that my island was somewhere off the coast of South America. Ships did not often come down this coast, and I said to myself, "I'm going to be on this island for a long time." So, on a long piece of wood, I cut these words:

I CAME HERE ON 30TH SEPTEMBER 1659

After that, I decided to make a *cut* for each day.

目睹了这一切，我非常悲伤。"为什么我活着，而我所有的朋友们却都死了？"我问自己。"现在对于我又会有什么事情发生呢？没有朋友独自生活在岛上，我怎么才能够逃离这儿？"

但随即我告诉自己我是幸运的——能够幸运地活下来，幸运有食物、有工具，幸运自己还年轻力壮。但我知道我的小岛在远离南美海岸的某个地方。船只不太经常沿着这个海岸航行，我对自己说，"我会在这个岛上待很长时间。"于是，在一长条的木牌上，我刻下了这些话：

我于1659年9月30日来到此岛。

以后，我决定每天都刻上一个记号。

---

cut *n.* 切口

Chater 5 Learning to Live Alone

I still needed a lot of things. "Well," I said, "I'm going to have to make them." So, every day, I worked.

First of all, I wanted to make my cave bigger. I carried out stone from the cave, and after many days' hard work I had a large cave in the side of the hill. Then I needed a table and a chair, and that was my next job. I had to work on them for a long time. I also wanted to make places to put all my food, and all my tools and guns. But every time I wanted a piece of wood, I had to *cut down* a tree. It was long, slow, difficult work, and during the next months I learnt to be very clever with my tools. There was no hurry. I had all the time in the world.

第五章 学会独自生活

我仍需要很多东西。"好吧，"我说，"我只能去做出来。"于是，每天，我都工作着。

首先，把我的山洞扩大。我从洞里运出石头，经过许多天的艰苦劳动，在小山的一侧有了个大的山洞。然后，我需要一张桌子和一把椅子，这便是我接下来的工作。为此，我不得不长时间地干。我还想要找些地方存放我的食物，以及我全部的工具和枪支。每一次我需要一块木板时都不得不砍倒一棵树。这是一项漫长艰难的工作，在随后的几个月里我学会熟

---

cut down 砍倒

I also went out every day, and I always had my gun with me. Sometimes I killed a wild animal, and then I had meat to eat.

But when it got dark, I had to go to bed because I had no light. I couldn't read or write because I couldn't see. For a long time, I didn't know what to do. But in the end, I learnt how to use the fat of dead animals to make a light.

The weather on my island was usually very hot, and there were often storms and heavy rain. The next June, it rained all the time, and I couldn't go out very often. I was also ill for some weeks, but slowly, I got better. When I was stronger, I began to go out again.

The first time I killed a wild animal, and the second time I caught a big *turtle*.

练地使用工具了。无须焦急，我拥有世界上的全部时间。

我依然每天出去，而且总是随身带枪。有时我杀死一只野兽，然后，就可以有肉吃了。

但每到天黑，因为没有灯，我就只好睡觉。由于看不见我不能读书也没法写字。好长一段时间我不知道该怎么做。但最终我学会了如何使用死兽的脂肪来点灯。

岛上的天气通常很热，经常有暴风雨。第二年的六月一直在下雨，我不能够经常出去。我也病了几个星期，但慢慢地我好转了。当我强壮起来时，我又开始外出。

第一次我杀了一只野兽，第二回我捕获了一只大海龟。

---

turtle *n.* 海龟

I was on the island for ten months before I visited other parts of it. During those months I worked hard on my cave and my house and my fence. Now I was ready to find out more about the rest of the island.

First, I walked along the side of a little river. There, I found open ground without trees.

Later, I came to more trees with many different fruits. I decided to take a lot of the fruit, and to put it to dry in the sun for a time. Then I could keep it for many months.

That night I went to sleep in a tree for the second time, and the next day I went on with my *journey*. Soon I came to an opening in the hills. In front of me, everything was green, and there were flowers

---

当我去参观岛的其他地方时，我在岛上已有10个月了。在这期间，我为我的洞穴、我的房子、我的篱笆忙活，现在我可以进一步了解该岛其他地方的情况了。

首先，我沿着一条小河岸前行。那儿，我发现一片没有树木的开阔地。

随后，我到达了一片结着各种水果的树林。我决定多摘些果子把它们在太阳下放一阵晒干。然后就可以保存很多个月了。

那个晚上，我第二次睡在了树上，第二天便又继续我的旅行。不久，我到了这个小山的开阔地。在我面前，一片郁郁葱葱，鲜花遍野。还有很

---

journey *n.* 旅行

everywhere. There were also a lot of different birds and animals. I saw that my house was on the worst side of the island. But I didn't want to move from there. It was my home now. I stayed away for three days, and then I came home. But I often went back to the other, greener side of the island.

And so my life went on. Every month I learnt to do or to make something new. But I had troubles and *accidents* too. Once there was a terrible storm with very heavy rain. The roof of my cave fell in, and nearly killed me! I had to build it up again with many pieces of wood.

I had a lot of food now. I cooked it over a fire or dried it in the sun. So I always had meat during the rainy months when I could not

多各种各样的鸟类和动物。我明白我的房子是在这个岛的最糟的一侧。但我并不打算从那儿迁移。那是我的家。我在外待了三天，然后回了家。但我经常回到这岛另一边，那里郁郁葱葱。

我的生活继续着。每个月我学会干点或制造点新的东西。但也总有麻烦和灾祸。一次一场夹着大雨的风暴来临。我的山洞的顶层塌了下来，差点就送了我的命！我不得不用很多木材把它重新建好。

现在，我有了很多食物。我把它架在火上烤或搁在太阳下晒干。因此，即使在雨季我不能够带枪外出时我也总有肉吃了。我学会做陶罐存放我的食物。但我非常想要做一个更坚固的罐子——一个放在火里不会破裂

accident *n.* 事故

go out with a gun. I learnt to make pots to keep my food in. But I wanted very much to make a harder, stronger pot—a pot that would not break in a fire. I tried many times, but I could not do it. Then one day I was lucky. I made some new *pots* and put them in a very hot fire. They changed colour, but did not break. I left them there for many hours, and when they were cold again, I found that they were hard and strong. That night I was very happy. I had hot water for the first time on the island.

By then, I also had my own bread. That was luck, too. One day I found a little bag. We used it on the ship, to keep the chickens' food in. There was still some of the food in the bag, and I dropped some of it onto the ground. A month later I saw something bright green there, and after six months I had a very small field of corn. I was very

的罐子。我试了很多次，可我没有成功。但有一天我太走运了。我制了几个新的罐子把它们搁在旺火里。它们变了颜色但却没有碎裂。我把它们放在那儿好几个小时，当它们再次冷却下来时，我发现它们既坚硬又牢固。那个晚上，我非常高兴。在这岛上我第一次喝到了热水。

从那时起，我也有了自己的面包。这也是一件幸运的事。一天我找到一个小袋子。在船上时我们用它来存放小鸡的饲料。在那袋子里还一直放着些食物，我把它们全倒在了地上。一个月后，我看见一些亮绿的幼苗，六个月后我便有了一块非常小的庄稼地。我很激动。

pot *n.* 罐

excited.

Perhaps now I could make my own bread!

It was easy to say, but not so easy to do. It is a lot of work to make bread from *corn*.

Many people eat bread, but how many people can take corn from a field and make bread out of it without help? I had to learn and to make many new things, and it was a year before I cooked and ate my first bread.

During all this time I never stopped thinking about escape. When I travelled across to the other side of the island, I could see the other islands, and I said to myself, "Perhaps I can get there with a boat. Perhaps I can get back to England one day."

So I decided to make myself a boat. I cut down a big tree, and

---

或许现在我可以做自己的面包了！

这些事说起来容易做起来却很困难。从谷物到面包需要很多工作。

很多人吃面包，但又有多少人可以无须帮助地种出谷物又做出面包呢？我不得不学着去做而且去做很多新的东西，在我烧出并食用我第一个面包时又一年过去了。

在这期间，我从来没有停止设法逃离小岛。当我纵深探索小岛的另外一侧时，我能够看见其他的小岛，我对自己说，"或许我用一只小船可以到达那儿。也许，有一天我便可以回到英格兰了。"

于是，我决定造自己的小船。我砍倒了一棵大树，然后开始掏成一个

---

corn *n.* 谷物

then began to make a long hole in it. It was hard work, but about six months later, I had a very fine canoe. Next, I had to get it down to the sea. How *stupid* I was! Why didn't I think before I began work? Of course, the canoe was too heavy. I couldn't move it! I pulled and pushed and tried everything, but it didn't move. I was very unhappy for a long time after that.

That happened in my fourth year on the island. In my sixth year I did make myself a smaller canoe, but I did not try to escape in it. The boat was too small for a long journey, and I did not want to die at sea. The island was my home now, not my prison, and I was just happy to be alive. A year or two later, I made myself a second canoe

---

长条形洞。这是很苦的工作，但六个月后，我就有了一只很好的独木舟。接下去，我必须让它下水。我是多么愚蠢啊！为什么开始工作前却没想到呢？毫无疑问，这只独木舟太重了。我不能够移得动它！我又拉又推用尽一切方法，但它却纹丝不动。这以后很长一段日子我都不开心。

造船是发生在我到岛上之后的第四个年头。在我的第六年里我又造了一只更小的船，但我没有用它来试图逃离。要想长途航行，这船太小了，我可不想死在海上。现在这岛便是我的家而非我的监狱，我相当快乐地生活着。一年或两年后，我在岛的另一侧又造了一只独木舟。我还在那儿建了第二座房子，所以我有了两个家。

---

stupid *adj.* 愚蠢的

on the other side of the island. I also built myself a second house there, and so I had two homes.

My life was still busy from morning to night. There were always things to do or to make. I learnt to make new clothes for myself from the skins of dead animals. They looked very strange, it is true, but they kept me dry in the rain.

I kept food and tools at both my houses, and also wild goats. There were many goats on the island, and I made fields with high fences to keep them in. They learnt to take food from me, and soon I had goat's milk to drink every day. I also worked hard in my *cornfields*. And so many years went by.

　　我的生活总是从早忙到晚，总是有很多事情要做。我学会用兽皮给自己做新衣服，虽然看起来挺古怪，但在雨季穿着它能使我保持干燥。

　　我在我的两所房子里都储放了食物和工具，也都养了野山羊。在这个岛上有很多野山羊，我用高栅栏圈了块地把它们围在里面。它们学会了从我这儿找食物，于是不久，我就每天有了羊奶喝。我同时也还在我的地里辛苦耕耘。于是，很多年就这样过去。

---

cornfield *n.* 玉米田

Chater 6 A Footprint

Then, one year, something strange and terrible happened. I often walked along the shore, and one day I saw something in the *sand*. I went over to look at it more carefully, and stopped in sudden surprise.

It was a footprint—the footprint of a man!

Who could this be? Afraid, I looked around me. I listened. I waited. Nothing. I was more and more afraid. Perhaps this man was one of those wild people who killed and ate other men! I looked everywhere, but there was nobody, and no other footprint. I turned and hurried home. "There's someone on my island," I said to myself.

第六章 一个脚印

有一年，古怪而且可怕的事情发生了。我经常沿着海岸走，一天我看见在沙滩上有些东西。我跑过去想瞧个仔细，但却在震惊中停了下来。

那是一个脚印———个人的脚印！

这是谁的呢？我害怕极了，环顾四周。我倾听着、等候着，却什么也没有，我越来越怕。也许，这是一个杀死并吃掉其他人的野人！我到处看，但都没有人，也没有别的脚印。我转过身匆忙赶回家。"岛上

---

sand *n.* 沙滩

"Perhaps he knows about me...Perhaps he's watching me now from behind a tree...Perhaps he wants to kill me."

That night I couldn't sleep. The next day I got all my guns ready and I put more wood and young trees around my house. Nobody could see me now. But, after fifteen years alone on the island, I was afraid, and I did not leave my *cave* for three days.

In the end, I had to go out to milk my goats. But for two years I was afraid. I stayed near my home and I never used my guns because I didn't want to make a noise. I could not forget the footprint, but I saw and heard nothing more, and slowly I began to feel happier.

有人，"我自言自语。"也许他知道我……也许他现在正从树后面观察我……也许他想杀了我。"

那一夜我不能入睡。第二天我把所有的枪备好并在房子的周围堆上更多的木头和小树。现在没有人能够看见我。可是，岛上独自生活了十五年后，我还是害怕，以至于一连三天没离开过我的山洞。

最终，我还是不得不出去给我的山羊挤奶，但两年里我一直提心吊胆。我待在房子的附近，从来不使用我的枪因为我不想弄出声音。我忘不掉那个脚印，但由于再也没有听到其他什么，渐渐地，我的感觉开始好起来。

---

cave *n.* 洞穴

One day, a year later, I was over on the west side of the island. From there I could see the other islands, and I could also see a boat, far out to sea. "If you have a boat, "I thought, "it's easy to sail across to this island. Perhaps that explains the footprint—it was a visitor from one of the other islands."

I began to move more *freely* around the island again, and built myself a third house. It was a very secret place in a cave. "No wild man will ever find that," I said to myself.

Then one year something happened which I can never forget. I was again on the west side of the island and was walking along the shore. Suddenly, I saw something which made me feel ill. There were heads, arms, feet, and other pieces of men's bodies everywhere. For

---

一年以后的一天，我来到小岛的西侧。从那儿我能看到其他岛和远处大海中的船。"如果有一只船，"我想，"穿过海面来到这个岛是挺容易。也许，这样可以解释这脚印——是一个来自其他岛的来访者。"

我又开始在岛上自由自在地走动并给自己建了第三所房子。它是在一个山洞里非常隐蔽的地方。"没有野人能够找到它，"我对自己说。

然而有一年，有些事的出现令我永远不能忘记。我又一次在岛的西侧沿着海岸散步。突然，我瞧见令我作呕的东西，那儿到处是人头、手臂、脚和一些人体其他部位的碎块。那一刻我简直无法思考，随即，我就明白了。以前另一个岛上的野人之间发生了一场战斗，然后他们带着他们的俘

---

freely *adv.* 自由自在地

a minute, I couldn't think, and then I understood. Sometimes there were fights between the *wild* men on the other islands. Then they came here to my island with their prisoners, to kill them, cook them, and eat them. Slowly, I went home, but I was very angry. How could men do this?

For many months I watched carefully for the smoke from fires, but I didn't see anything.

Somehow the wild men came and went, and I never saw them. I was angry and afraid. I wanted to shoot them all, but there were many of them and only one of me. "Perhaps I can shoot two or

---

虏来到了我的岛上，杀了俘虏，接着烹了吃掉。慢慢地，我走回家中，我愤怒。人怎么能够做这样的事？

几个月来，我仔细观察火堆升起的烟，但我什么也没看见。

究竟野人如何来来去去我却从来没有发现过。我又愤怒又害怕。我想把他们全都杀了，但他们有很多人而我只有一个人。"也许，我可以杀死

---

wild *adj.* 野蛮的

three," I said to myself, "but then they will kill and eat me."

Then, one morning in my twenty-third year on the island, I was out in my fields and I saw the *smoke* from a fire. Quickly, I went up the hill to watch.

There were nine men around the fire, and they were cooking their terrible food. Then these wild men danced round the fire, singing and shouting. This went on for about two hours, and then they got into their boats and sailed away. I went down to the shore and saw the blood of the dead men on the sand. "The next time they come, I'm going to kill them," I said angrily.

两三个，"我自言自语，"可是，然后他们却会杀了我并把我吃掉。"

此后，正是我在岛上的第23个年头的一个早上，我正在我的地里劳作，我看见一堆火上升起的烟。飞快地，我爬上山去观察。

有9个人围绕着火堆，正在烹煮着可怕的食物。接着那些野人围绕着火堆跳起了舞，唱着欢呼着。这样整整持续了两个小时，然后他们上了小船离去。我来到海滩上，目睹了沙滩上死人的淋漓鲜血。"下次他们来，我一定会杀了他们，"我愤怒地说。

smoke *n.* 烟

Chater 7 Man Friday

For two years I never went anywhere without my gun. I felt lonely and afraid, and had many *sleepless* nights. One night there was a very bad storm, and I thought I heard the sound of guns out at sea. The next morning I looked out, and saw a ship. It was lying on its side not far from the shore. Quickly, I put my little boat in the water and sailed out to it.

There were two dead men on the ship, but no one alive. The bodies of the other sailors were lost in the sea. I took some clothes and tools, and also a box of Spanish gold and silver money. I was a rich man now, but what use was money to me? I could not buy anything with it.

第七章 星期五

两年来，没带枪我从不四处乱走。我感到孤独和害怕，许多晚上无法入睡。一个晚上来了一场非常厉害的风暴，我想我听到海上的枪声。第二天早晨我往外望去，看到一只轮船斜搁在离海岸不远的海面上。我迅速地把我的小船拖下水并朝大船驶去。

船上有两个死人，但没有人活着，其他水手的尸体都消失在海上。我带走一些衣服和工具，还有一箱西班牙金币和银币。现在我成了一个富翁，但这些钱对我有什么用呢？我用它们什么也买不到。

sleepless *adj.* 失眠的

I wanted people, a friend, somebody to talk to...somebody who could help me escape from my island. One morning I woke up and made a plan. "I'll try to catch one of the prisoners of the wild men," I said to myself. "He'll be happy to be *alive* and perhaps he'll help me to escape." I watched day and night, but for a year and a half there were no boats.

Then one day five boats came. There were about thirty men and they had two prisoners. They made their fire on the sand and danced round it. Then they killed one of the prisoners and began to cook their terrible meal. The second prisoner waited under the trees, with two men to watch him. Suddenly, the prisoner turned and ran. The two men ran after him, but the other wild men were busy round

我渴望人类，一个朋友，可以谈话的人……可以帮助我逃离孤岛的人。有天早上我醒来作了个计划。"我将试图救一个那些野人的俘虏，"我自言自语。"他将因为活着而高兴，可能他会帮助我逃跑。"我日夜观望着，但一年半过去了，却再也没见到船只出现。

有一天，海上来了五只船，大约有三十个人和两个俘虏。他们在沙滩上生火并围着火跳舞。然后他们杀了一个俘虏并开始煮可怕的食物。另一个俘虏在树下等候，留有两个人看守。突然，这个俘虏转身就跑。两个人在后面追赶，但其余的野人围着火忙着，并没有看见发生的事。

alive *adj.* 活着的

the fire and did not see what was happening.

The prisoner ran like a wild goat, and soon I saw that he was coming near the bottom of my hill. As fast as I could, I ran down the hill and jumped out of the trees between the prisoner and the two wild men. I hit the first man with the wooden end of my gun and he fell down, but I had to shoot the second man. The poor prisoner did not move. He was afraid of the noise of my gun.

I called to him and tried to show him that I was friendly. Slowly, he moved nearer to me, but just then the first wild man began to get up from the ground. Then the prisoner spoke and I understood that he wanted my sword. How happy I was to hear words again! I gave him my *sword*, and at once he cut off the head of his enemy.

那俘虏像一只野山羊在奔跑，不一会儿我看到他已跑到我的山脚下。我尽快地跑下山去，在俘虏和另两个野人之间的树丛里跳出来。我用木制的枪柄击倒第一个野人，但我却不得不开枪打死第二个。可怜的俘虏没有移动，他被枪声吓呆了。

我大声招呼他，努力向他表明我是友好的。他慢慢地向我靠近，但这时第一个野人开始从地上爬起来。然后这俘虏说话了，我明白他需要我的刀。能够听到人的语言我是多么高兴啊！我给他我的刀，他立刻砍掉了敌人的脑袋。

---

sword *n.* 剑；刀

Hurriedly, we hid the dead bodies under some leaves, and then left quickly. I took my prisoner to my secret cave on the other side of the island and gave him food and drink. After that, he went to sleep.

He was a fine young man, about twenty-five years old, tall and well-built, with a kind face and a nice smile. He had a brown skin, black hair, bright eyes and strong white teeth. I decided to give him the name of "Man Friday", because I first saw him on a Friday.

When he woke up in the morning, he ran out to me. I was milking my goats in the field, and he got down on the ground and put his head near my foot. I understood that he was thanking me, and I tried to show him that I was his friend.

　　我们急忙把尸体藏在了落叶下，然后迅速地离开。我把俘虏带到岛的另一面我隐蔽的洞穴，并给他食物和水，不久，他睡着了。

　　他是一个可爱的年轻人，大约25岁，身材高大健壮，和善的脸上带着开心的微笑。他褐色皮肤，黑头发，明亮的眼睛和坚固的白牙齿。我决定叫他"仆人星期五"，因为我是在星期五第一次见到他。

　　当他早上醒来时，他跑到我的身边。我正在田里挤羊奶，他蹲在地上把他的头贴在我的脚边。我明白他在感谢我，我努力向他表明我是他的朋友。

---

hurriedly *adv.* 匆忙地

I began to teach him to speak English, and soon he could say his name, "Master", and "Yes" and "No". How good it was to hear a man's voice again!

Later that day we went back to my first house. We went carefully along the beach, but there were no boats and no wild men. Just blood and *bones* all over the sand. I felt ill, but Friday wanted to eat the pieces of men's bodies which were still on the ground. I showed him that this was terrible for me, and he understood.

When we got to my house, I gave Man Friday some trousers, and I made him a coat and a hat. He liked his new clothes very much. Then I made him a little tent to sleep in, but for a few weeks I always took my gun to bed with me. Perhaps Friday was still a wild man and would try to kill me in the night. At first, Friday was very afraid of my

---

我开始教他说英语，不久，他能够说他的名字，"主人"及"是"与"不是"。重新听到人的声音是多么美妙啊！

那天傍晚，我们回到我第一次建造的房子。我们沿着海滨小心走着，但那儿没有船和野人，只有血迹和尸骨散落在沙滩上，我感到恶心，但星期五想吃地上的尸体碎块，我向他表示这对我来说很可怕，他明白了。

当我们回到房子里，我给星期五几条裤子，而且给他做了件外套和一顶帽子，他非常喜欢他的新衣服。然后我给他搭了一座小帐篷睡觉，但一连几个星期我总是带枪睡觉，或许因为星期五还是一个野人，也许他会在夜里杀了我。开始，星期五害怕我的枪，有时他对枪说话，叫枪不要杀死他。

---

bone *n.* 骨头

gun. Sometimes he talked to it, and asked it not to kill him.

Friday was a quick learner and his English got better day by day. He helped me with the *goats* and with the work in the cornfields, and soon we were good friends. I enjoyed teaching him and, most of all, having a friend to talk to. This was the happiest of all my years on the island.

Friday and I lived together happily for three years. I told him the story of my adventures and about life in England, and he told me about his country and his people. One day we were at the top of the highest hill on the island, and we were looking out to sea. It was a very clear day and we could see a long way. Suddenly, Friday began to jump up and down, very excited.

　　星期五学得很快，他的英语讲得一天比一天好。他帮我养山羊和在田地里干活，不久我们成了好朋友。我乐于教他，最重要的是有一个朋友可以谈话，这是我在岛上最快乐的时光。

　　我和星期五幸福地一起生活了三年，我告诉他我的冒险经历和在英国的生活，他告诉我有关他的国家及人民。一天，我们站在岛的最高的山顶，眺望大海。天气十分晴朗，我们可以看得很远。突然，星期五上蹦下跳，非常兴奋。

---

goat *n.* 山羊

"'What's the matter?" I said.

"Look, Master, look!" Friday cried. "I can see my country. Look over there!" I looked, and there to the northwest, between the sea and the sky, was a long thin piece of land. I learnt later that it was the island of Trinidad, and that my island was in the mouth of the River Orinoco on the north *coast* of South America.

I began to think again about escape. Perhaps Friday wanted to go home too. Perhaps together we could get to his country. But what then? Would Friday still be my friend, or would his people kill me and eat me?

I took Friday to the other side of the island and showed him my

---

"发生了什么事？"我说。

"看，主人，看哪！"星期五叫起来。"我能看见我的国家。看，就在那儿！"我看到从这儿往西北，在海天之间，有一片狭长的土地。我后来知道这是特立尼达岛，而我的岛在南美洲北部海岸的奥里诺科河的河口。

我又重新开始考虑逃离。也许星期五也想回家。或许我们能一起回到他的国家。但那会怎样呢？星期五仍会是我的朋友吗？他的伙伴会杀死并吃掉我吗？

我把星期五带到岛的另一边，向他展示我庞大的独木舟。它仍躺在树下。现在它非常旧，木头上有些洞。

---

coast *n.* 海岸

big canoe. It still *lay* under the trees. It was very old now, and there were holes in the wood.

"Could a boat like this sail to your country, Friday?" I asked him.

"Oh yes," he answered. "A boat like this can carry a lot of food and drink."

"Then we'll make another canoe like it, and you can go home in it," I said.

But Friday looked very unhappy. "Why are you angry with me?" he asked. "What have I done? Why do you want to send me home?"

"But I thought you wanted to go home," I said.

"星期五，像这样的船能驶到你的国家吗？"我问他。

"噢，能，"他回答说。"像这样的船能装运许多食物和水。"

"那么我们将制造差不多的另一只独木舟，你就可以乘着它回家了，"我说。

但星期五看起来很不开心。"为什么你生我的气呢？"他问。"我做了什么？为什么你想送我回家？"

"但我认为你想回家，"我说道。

---

lie *v.* 躺

"Yes. But you must come with me. Kill me if you want, but don't send me away from you!"

Then I saw that Friday was a true friend, and so I agreed to go with him. We began work on the canoe at once. Friday *chose* the tree himself—he understood wood better than I did—and we cut it down. We worked hard and in a month the boat was finished. Two weeks later it was in the sea, and we began to get ready for our long journey.

"是的。但是你一定要和我一起去。假如你想杀我也可以，但不要把我送走！"

此后我发现星期五是一个真诚的朋友，因此我同意和他一起走。我们马上开始建造独木舟。星期五亲自挑选木头——他比我更懂得木材的好坏——我们砍倒树木。我们辛苦地工作，一个月就把船造好了。两个星期后船下水了，我们开始为长途旅行作准备。

choose *v.* 选择

Chater 8 Escape From the Island

I was now in my twenty-seventh year on the island, and I did not want to be there for another year. We worked hard to get the corn in, and to make a lot of bread. We had dried fruit and *salted* meat, and big pots to keep water in. One evening Friday went out to look for a turtle for meat and eggs. But in less than an hour he was back, and he looked very afraid.

"Master! Master!" he cried. "There's a great ship near the island, and men are coming to the shore in a boat!"

I jumped up and ran with him down to the shore. To my great

第八章 逃离孤岛

现在我在这岛上已经待了27年，我不愿再待下去了。我们勤劳地工作，收割谷物，制成许多面包。我们准备了干果、咸肉和装水的大罐子。一天傍晚，星期五为了吃肉和海龟蛋去抓海龟。但不到一个钟头他就回来了，他看起来非常害怕。

"主人！主人！"他叫喊着。"在岛的附近有一只大船，他们坐着一条小船上岸来了！"

我跳起来跟他一起下山朝岸边跑。令我非常惊奇的是，我看到那是

---

salted adj. 盐腌的

surprise, I saw that it was an English ship! But why was it here? English ships never came this way. Perhaps they were *pirates*! "Don't let them see you, Friday!" I called. "We'll hide in the trees and watch."

There were eleven men in the boat, but three of them were prisoners. Their arms were tied with rope, but their legs were free and they could walk. The other sailors pushed the three prisoners up the beach, laughing and shouting and hitting them. Then some of them sat down on the sand and began to drink. Others walked away to look at the island, and two men stayed to watch the boat. The three prisoners walked slowly along the beach and sat down under a tree, not far from us. They looked very unhappy.

Very quietly, I came up behind them through the trees, and called out to them in English.

一艘英国船！但为什么会在这儿？英国船只从不朝这个方向来。或许他们是海盗！"别让他们看见你，星期五！"我叫道。"我们躲到树后，瞧着。"

船上有11个人，但其中3个是俘虏。他们的手臂用绳子捆着，但他们的脚是自由的，可以走路。其他水手把这三个俘虏押到海滩上，笑着，叫着并踢他们。一些人坐在沙滩上开始喝酒。其他人走开去观察小岛，留下两个人看守小船。3个俘虏沿着海滩走得很慢，在离我们不远的树下坐了下来。他们显得非常沮丧。

我悄悄地穿过树丛走到他们后面，用英语招呼他们。

---

pirate *n.* 海盗

"Don't be afraid," I said. "I'm an Englishman. Perhaps I can help you."

The three men turned and looked at me. They did not answer at once; they were too surprised. Perhaps they thought I was a wild man myself, in my strange home-made clothes of animals' skins, and with my long hair and *beard*. Then the oldest man spoke.

"I am the captain of that ship," he said, "and these two men are my first and second officers. Last night there was a mutiny, and the seamen took the ship from me. Now they're going to leave the three of us here, to die on this island."

"Do these mutineers have guns?"

"Only two," he answered, "and they've left those on the boat."

"不要害怕，"我说。"我是英国人。或许我能帮助你们。"

这三个人转过身来看着我。他们没有马上回答，他们很惊讶。可能会认为我这个穿着用动物皮毛自制的古怪衣服，长长的头发和胡须的人是个野人。稍后，最年长的人说话了。

"我是船长，"他说，"这两个是我的大副和二副。昨晚发生了一场叛乱，水手夺走了我的船。现在他们将把我们三人丢在这儿，让我们死在岛上。"

"这些反叛者有枪么？"

"只有两支枪，"他回答，"他们把枪留在小船上了。"

---

beard *n.* 胡须

"All right," I said. "We'll fight them, but if we get your ship back for you, you must take me back to England."

The captain agreed immediately and thanked me very warmly for my help. Friday ran back to my house to get all the guns, and the captain and I made a plan.

The first part was easy because the seamen were not ready for a fight. We shot the two men at the boat, and the captain shot another man. This man, Tom Smith, was the worst of them all and he began the *mutiny* on the ship. Then the captain talked to the other five men, and they agreed to help him. They did not really want to be mutineers, but they were afraid of Tom Smith.

"Now," I said to the captain, "we must get back your ship. How

---

"好的，"我说。"我们来打他们，但是如果我们为你夺回了船，你们必须带我回英国去。"

船长立即同意并热情感谢我的帮助。星期五跑回房子取来所有的枪，船长和我作了计划。

第一步还是容易的，因为水手没有作战的准备。我们开枪打死了船上的两人，船长击毙了另一个。这个叫汤姆·史密斯的，是其中最坏的一个，他发动了这个船上的叛乱。然后船长和其他五个人谈话，他们答应帮助船长。他们并非真的想成为反叛者，只是他们畏惧汤姆·史密斯。

"现在，"我对船长说，"我们必须回到你的船上。船上有多少

---

mutiny n. 叛乱

many men are on it?"

"Twenty-six," the captain replied, "and they will fight hard because they won't want to go home. It is death for all mutineers in England. But not all the men are bad. I'm sure that some of them will help me."

Just then we saw another boat, which was coming from the ship to the shore. There were ten men in it, and they all had guns. We ran into the trees and waited.

It was a long hard fight, but by now it was dark and this helped us very much. We ran here and there in the trees, calling and shouting. The *seamen* could not see us and did not know how many men they were fighting. In the end the first officer shouted to them:

人？"

"26个，"船长回答，"他们会顽强抵抗，因为他们不想回家。在英国所有的反叛者都会处以死刑。但并非所有的人都坏。我相信有一些人会帮助我的。"

这时我们看见另一只小船，正离开大船向岸边驶来。船上有10个人，他们都带了枪。我们跑进树丛等着。

这是一场艰苦的持久战，但此刻天已黑了，这对我们很有利。我们在树丛里到处跑，叫喊着。水手们看不见我们也不知道和他们打仗的有多少人。最后，大副朝他们喊：

---

seaman *n.* 水手

"Put down your guns and stop fighting! The captain has fifty island people to help him. We can kill you all!"

So the seamen stopped fighting and we took their guns. Three of the men agreed to come back to the captain, and we put the others in my cave. Friday and I stayed to watch the prisoners, while the captain and his men went back to *fight for* the ship.

All night we listened to the sound of guns and shouting, but in the morning, when the sun came up, the captain was master of his ship again. I went down to the shore to meet him.

"My dear friend," he cried, "There's your ship! I'll take you to the ends of the world in it!"

"放下武器。停止战斗！船长得到了50名岛上居民的帮助。我们能把你们全部消灭！"

因此水手们停止了作战，我们缴了他们的枪。其中3人同意回到船长这边，我们把其余的人送进我的山洞里。我和星期五留下看守俘虏，而船长和他的手下回去为夺船而战斗。

整夜我们听见枪声及叫喊声，但到了早晨，当太阳升起时，船长又成了大船的主人。我下山到海岸边去迎接他。

"我亲爱的朋友，"他喊道。"那是你的船！我会用它把你载到世界

---

fight for　为……而战斗

I put my arms round him, and we laughed and cried together. How happy I was to leave the island!

My good friend Friday came with me, of course, but we left the *mutineers* on the island.

We decided not to kill them; they could begin a new life on the island. I showed them my three houses, my cornfields and my goats, and all my tools. Their life would he easy because of all my hard work for so many years.

And so, on the nineteenth of December 1689—after twenty-seven years, two months and nineteen days—I said good-bye to my island and sailed home to England.

的每个角落！"

我拥抱他，我们一起笑着欢呼着。离开这个小岛我是多么高兴啊！

我的好朋友星期五当然跟随着我，但我们把那些叛乱者留在了岛上。

我们决定不杀他们，他们能够在岛上开始一种新的生活。我给他们看了我的三间房子，我的庄稼地和我的山羊以及所有的工具。由于我多年的艰苦劳动他们的生活会轻松得多。

于是，在1689年12月19日——经过了27年2个月19天——我告别了我的小岛，乘船返回了英国。

---

mutineer *n.* 叛乱者

Chater 9 Home in England

When I came back to England, I felt like a *stranger* in the country. Many things were different, and not many people remembered me. I went home to York, but my father and mother were dead, and also my two brothers. I did find the two sons of one of my brothers. They were happy to learn that I was alive, and I was pleased to find some family.

After some months I decided to go down to Lisbon in Portugal. I had friends there who could help me to sell my land in Brazil, and I needed the money. Friday came with me.

第九章 英国的家

当我回到英格兰，我觉得自己好像是这个国家的一个陌生客人。许多东西都变了样，没有几个人能记得我。我回到约克郡的家，我的父母亲及我两个兄弟都已去世了。我找到了我一个兄弟的两个儿子。知道我还活着他们非常高兴，我很高兴找到了一些家人。

过了几个月我决定去葡萄牙的里斯本。我有些朋友在那儿可以帮我卖掉在巴西的土地，我需要钱。星期五和我一起去。

---

stranger *n.* 陌生人

He was always a good and true friend to me. In Lisbon I found the Portuguese captain, who took me in his ship to Brazil, all those years ago. It was good to see him again, and he helped me with my business. Soon I was ready to go home again—by land. No more adventures and dangers by sea for me!

It was a long, hard journey. We had to cross the mountains between Spain and France in winter, and the snow was deep. Poor Friday was very afraid of the snow. In his country it was always hot, and he did not like cold weather.

Back in England I found a house and began to live a quiet life. My two *nephews* came to live with me. The younger one wanted to be

---

他一直是我的一位忠实的好朋友。在里斯本我找到了多年前带我去巴西的葡萄牙船长。再次见到他真是太好了，他帮助我做生意。不久我又准备回家——是经陆路。对我来说在海上航行已没有更多的冒险和危险！

这是一次长途跋涉的旅行。我们不得不在冬天穿越位于西班牙和法国之间的大山，积雪很深。可怜的星期五非常害怕雪。在他的国家天气总是很热，他不喜欢寒冷的天气。

回到英国我找了座房子，开始过平静的生活。我的两个侄子来和我

---

nephew *n.* 侄子

a sailor, and so I found him a place on a ship. *After a while* I married, and had three children, two sons and a daughter. Then my wife died, and my nephew, who was now the captain of a ship, came home to see me. He knew that I did not really like a quiet life.

"I have a fine ship, uncle," he said. "I'm going out to the East Indies—India, Malaya, the Philippines...Why don't you come with me?"

And so, in 1694, I went to sea again, and had many more adventures. Perhaps one day I'll write another book about them.

住在一起。小的一个想做一名水手，于是我给他在船上找了个职位。过了不久我结婚了，生了三个孩子，两个儿子和一个女儿。后来我的妻子去世了，我的那个侄子回家看我，他现在已当了船长。他知道我并不真正喜欢平静的生活。

"我有一艘好船，叔叔，"他说。"我将去东印度群岛——印度、马来西亚、菲律宾……为什么你不同我一起去呢？"

于是，1694年，我再次出海，有了更多冒险的经历。或许有一天我会另外写一本关于它们的书。

---

after a while   不久